The Harvard Black Rock Forest

SIGHTLINE BOOKS

The Iowa Series in Literary Nonfiction

Patricia Hampl & Carl H. Klaus, series editors

The Harvard

Black Rock Forest

GEORGE W. S. TROW

University of Iowa Press Ψ Iowa City

University of Iowa Press, Iowa City 52242
Originally published in the *New Yorker*, June 11, 1984
Published here by permission
Printed in the United States of America
Design by Richard Hendel
http://www.uiowa.edu/uiowapress

The University of Iowa is a member of Green Press Initiative and is
committed to preserving natural resources. This book has been
printed on paper that is 60 percent recycled. GPI is a nonprofit
program dedicated to saving trees and natural resources through
increasing the use of recycled paper in the book-publishing sector.

Printed on acid-free paper

Library of Congress Cataloging-in-Publication Data
Trow, George W. S.
The Harvard Black Rock Forest / George W. S. Trow.
p.   cm.—(Sightline books)
Originally published in the New Yorker, June 11, 1984.
ISBN 0-87745-895-2 (pbk.)
1. Black Rock Forest (N.Y.)—History.   I. Title.   II. Series.
SD358.8.N7T76 2004
333.75'09747'31—dc22   2003063417

04 05 06 07 08 P 5 4 3 2 1

The Harvard Black Rock Forest

It is my plan to begin in the middle of things, with a man alone on a tract of land. It is 1892. The man is young and healthy; the land has been damaged. The young man is a forester, hired to work on this land. Now he is joined by a second young man, the owner of the land — a young man who is enormously rich. Together they look around at the tract of damaged land, which could have been damaged by anyone; then they look up at a house that is being built. It is an astonishing house: only a rich person could build it.

All the rest of this essay takes place within the set of circumstances I have just described: two friends, one a forester, one an enormously rich young man, looking first at a large tract of damaged land and then at an astonishing limestone palace.

The young man alone on the tract of land is Gifford Pinchot, the first American to be trained as a forester, and, I think, one of the important men in the history of the United States. The young man who joins him is George Washington Vanderbilt, of that rich family. As an old man, Gifford Pinchot wrote a description of George Washington Vanderbilt as he was at the time of the building of the limestone house, called Biltmore:

> George was a lover of art and of the great outdoors, a slim, simple, and rather shy young man, too much and too long sheltered by female relatives. . . . Biltmore was his heart's delight.

Pinchot described the tract of land, near Asheville, North Carolina:

Biltmore Estate covered a little over 7000 acres of rolling hills and bottom lands on both sides of the French Broad River. Half of it was woodland. It had been put together from small impoverished farms, the forest on which had been burned, slashed, and overgrazed until it was little more than the shadow of its former self. In Europe I had seen nothing like it, but millions of acres east of the Mississippi were its brothers and sisters.

Pinchot described the limestone house:

Biltmore House, the center of the Vanderbilt estate, not yet completed when I saw it first, was a magnificent château of Indiana limestone. With the terrace and stables it was a thousand feet in length. Its setting was superb, the view from it breathtaking, and as a feudal castle it would have been beyond criticism, and perhaps beyond praise.

But in the United States of the nineteenth century and among the one-room cabins of the Appalachian mountaineers, it did not belong. The contrast was a devastating commentary on the injustice of concentrated wealth. Even in the early nineties I had sense enough to see that.

The rich young man who had the palace built, however, also put his forest under management. Pinchot wrote:

Here was my chance. Biltmore could be made to prove what America did not yet understand, that trees could be cut and the forest preserved at one and the same time.

When I said that I thought that Gifford Pinchot was one of the important men in the history of the United States, I was thinking not only of his importance in the history of forestry and conservation but, even more, of his quality of mind. He was an *amateur*. At all moments in his career, he was fond of wearing a wide-brimmed slouch hat that made him look like a Westerner and an Easterner both. At all moments in his career, he failed to please one professional or another who was in possession of: the *facts* — political, scientific, or practical. Now we are living with a hunger for certainty. We want to be *certain*. Or, rather, we are hungry for certainty, but, despairing of attaining it ourselves, we want to know that someone else is certain. If this should change — that is, if we allow ourselves to doubt consciously whether we can be certain — we may need to try to regain an understanding of how men like Gifford Pinchot looked at American life.

One thing Gifford Pinchot understood was that in America an effective man must not blame farmers who damage their land or very rich young men who want to build (and sometimes do build) limestone palaces. He may have learned some part of this from Frederick Law Olmsted, the landscape architect, who also worked at Biltmore, and who guided and encouraged him. "It was Mr. Olmsted who was responsible for the plan to make Biltmore Estate the nest egg for practical Forestry in America," Pinchot wrote, and he explained:

> Mr. Olmsted was to me one of the men of the century. He was a quiet-spoken little lame man with a most magnificent head and one of the best minds I have ever had the good luck to encounter. His knowledge was far wider than his profession. He knew the territory of the United States as few men knew it, and he was full of stories of early days. For instance:
>
> Riding into Sacramento, California one day in the early fifties, Mr. Olmsted noticed a single figure standing out in the open plaza. The figure in the plaza was amusing himself by taking pot shots with a pistol at every man he saw. Presently a man walked straight out to the shooter, who was shouting, raging drunk, and took his gun away.
>
> The man who did this bravest thing was a gambler who had given clothes taken from smallpox victims to peaceful and harmless Digger Indians — a form of murder as low and contemptible as the gambler's courage was high and fine.
>
> That story did me a lot of good. It shed a light on human nature that has helped me ever since not to underestimate people I don't like.

THE DUAL HIERARCHY WE LIVE IN

Everyone lives somewhere, but not everyone feels that he is living in one particular place. The man on the street with an earphone-connected-to-music in his ear — where is he living? Even ambitious people have, in recent times, wanted to overcome the limitations implicit in living in one place. Already, I need a distinction: between the person who is thoughtlessly impelled to place a popular-culture webbing over the place where he is and the person who sees that his work, when it is most successful, is everywhere and nowhere. Both persons have noticed that when an event is merely *somewhere* it has failed.

To be successful now, one would want to be a person whose work was dispersed throughout the world but who lived (nevertheless) in a collegial atmosphere. Scientists and entertainers do this. It is the work of scientists and entertainers which has been most thoroughly dispersed throughout the modern world, and yet scientists and entertainers live in a collegial atmosphere, within which the work of an ambitious man is likely to be known to another ambitious man. Thus, history survives within the history of science and the history of entertainment — especially the history of entertainment on film. Silent films, vaudeville turns, and the work of B-picture directors are studied by men who do not intend to do vaudeville or direct B pictures or make pictures without sound. In the same way, scientists know and make use of the work of men whose theories have been overthrown.

A collegial situation in which a sense of history leads men to respect work a layman would ignore is rare now. The collegial atmosphere around the work of lawyers is thinner than it used to be, and around the work of literary men it is very thin; this is a measure of the loss of vitality in these two spheres. Traditions are maintained by collegial bodies that retain vitality and direct part of their vital energy to the protection of parts of themselves which would be ignored by a layman. Americans are not, as is sometimes said, a people without traditions; our traditions are being formed within science and entertainment.

The vast majority of people do not see evidence of a collegial enterprise in what they encounter either on the surface of life (where the history of science is to be seen) or in their dreams (formed by entertainment). The world is not familiar from the point of view of knowledge; nor does its mystery give birth to healthy aspirations. Rather, the lives of most people are characterized by attempts to make the world familiar through the application of affection, and by nonsensical aspirations: attempts to reach images in the air and to take part in events in the sky.

But scientists and entertainers do see evidence of sense and of a collegial spirit in what is around them, and this convinces them that there is more structure in the lives of people than there really is. Consider the example of a filmmaker whose film about gangsters is being shown on television. He knows the film, of course, and he knows other films of the genre, and he knows how television works; that is, he could explain how his film came to be shown on television and what people were involved. He may not know anything about gangsters; that doesn't matter. He himself may be capable of being fooled by some of his own work (he may be imitating the work of other, greater men, whose work he is incapable of understanding), but a partial delusion does not make the experience of watching the film a crazy one for him: he may even transform what does not make sense into a sensible ambition to know and do more. For him, the explicable and the mysterious are *in contact*, as they are for all men who are involved in a ritual and are taking it seriously.

For a child, the experience of watching this film is completely different. The explicable and the mysterious are not in contact. The mystery that the film-maker consciously refers to in his film and the mystery of which he is not conscious (his delusion: the result of not understanding his own work) — these mysteries are not important, or even perceptible, to the child, who is under the weight of the questions "What is television?" and "How does something *get on* television?" One definition of a ritual would be: a circumstance in which images fall into an order that makes deep sense. One definition of television would be: an unsuccessful ritual; or a ritual that works only for the priests.

Science, like entertainment, is found in layers, in a hierarchy, throughout the world. From a scientific point of view, there are important connections between the most repellent application of a degraded technology and the most sublime speculation. This being true, the consequences of the degraded technology are, perhaps, slightly less repellent to a scientist than they would be to a sensitive nonscientist. What joins the scientist and the entertainer is this: they create the modern world but do not live in it, while other people live in it without knowing much about how it has been made.

WITHIN AN OLDER HIERARCHY

In the back seat of an automobile travelling south on Route 9W in the small, decayed city of Newburgh, on the west bank of the Hudson, Hamilton Fish, of that distinguished New York family, Harvard Class of 1910, former member of Congress, said to the air in front of him, "I have too much money now. I'm embarrassed." It is the habit of some people whose final reference is to certainty to speak to the air in front of them. "It's true," Mr. Fish said. "I'm embarrassed." It was not true.

Mr. Fish was referring to his third wife, who is rich and with whom he was at this moment living in a nineteenth-century house overlooking the Hudson near Newburgh. This was a change for Mr. Fish, whose family has had strong connections in Garrison, over on the east bank of the river. The Newburgh house is handsome on the outside. Inside, it is opulent. The house is surrounded by specimen trees. Each tree carries a small tag giving its proper name, or is meant to carry one. "Still," Mr. Fish said, into the air, "charity can be very dangerous. My first wife's father gave a great deal of money to Williams College and then had very little left for himself." Mr. Fish opened his eyes wide, and so opened wide his big face. This he did to add emphasis to the words "had very little left for himself." Mr. Fish, in his nineties, is extremely handsome — tall, with a famous nose and famous eyes. His late sister Rosalind Fish Cutler had eyes even bigger, the wonder of her friends and family, but Mr. Fish's career has been public, so his eyes are better known.

Travelling south on 9W, the automobile crossed the principal thoroughfare of the small, decayed city of Newburgh. There was silence in the automobile as it crossed this strong street, which is called Broadway. Broadway is a boulevard, eighty-two feet wide. After crossing Broadway, the automobile followed the dispersal of the small city of Newburgh.

After a time, a man in the front seat said, "Do you think Newburgh will come back, Uncle Ham?"

"No," Mr. Fish said.

Route 9W proceeds south of Newburgh through the old town of New Windsor and into the Hudson Highlands. When one is travelling south, Storm King Mountain is off to the left. To the right is the Harvard Black Rock Forest, a tract of thirty-eight hundred acres which was developed as a scientific, or demonstration, forest by Dr. Ernest G. Stillman, a benefactor of Harvard; he endowed the forest and left it to Harvard at his death, in 1949. Farther south, a traveller may turn off to the United States Military

Academy, at West Point. The Hudson Highlands are merely fifty miles from New York City, but there are large tracts of undeveloped land here: within the West Point Military Reservation; within Storm King State Park, which is a part of the Palisades Interstate Park; and within the Harvard Black Rock Forest.

Of Harvard and its relationship to the Black Rock Forest, to the Stillman family of benefactors, to the science of silviculture (within a demonstration forest), it should be said that, in response to the *new, tough reality* in American life, Harvard University has been looking closely, ruthlessly at its assets. Where an asset *does not perform*, it is suspect. Recently, Harvard University decided that the Black Rock Forest, the tract of thirty-eight hundred acres within the Hudson Highlands given to it by Dr. Ernest Stillman (a benefactor from a family of benefactors), *had not performed* and should be sold. There were difficulties. It was not possible to say that the forest was a *burden*, for instance. The expenses of upkeep were light; there were no large buildings in the forest; *runaway fuel costs* and other such aspects of the new, tough reality were absent. Expenses had not outstripped income. Most emphatically, they had not. Income rose and rose and rose. At moments, it must have been embarrassing how much money Harvard had available to be spent within the forest. This money derived from a fund established by Dr. Ernest Stillman primarily to support the expenses of maintaining the forest and the expenses of conducting scientific work within the forest; the fund amounted to about a million dollars at the time of Dr. Stillman's death, in 1949. It amounts to more than that now. Harvard has said that although it is not possible for Harvard to keep the forest it is possible for it to keep the money.

🐦 🐦 🐦

Hamilton Fish (Harvard '10) and his companions were on their way to a meeting of Harvard men. Their trip took them through the old, decayed city of Newburgh and through the Hudson Highlands — where the Black Rock Forest is. The meeting was a *fund-raiser*, connected to an effort by the President and Fellows of Harvard College to raise (at first; they asked for a hundred million more later) the sum of two hundred and fifty million dollars. It was held at a hotel on the grounds of the United States Military Academy. There was a view of the Hudson River (very narrow here). There were talks by three men, and there was a film.

🐦 🐦 🐦

The collegial atmosphere around the men of Harvard is thin now. It is thinner than the atmosphere around lawyers, not so thin as the atmosphere around literary people. It becomes thick, richer in oxygen, more nearly capable of sustaining life, during fund-raising periods. Men are injected into buildings; their money is mortar. Buildings reveal that they were built by men and have always housed people. Everything is named. "The Names of Harvard" is a booklet issued at this fund-raising period to set out the details of the process by which money becomes mortar and mortar is trained to speak the name of some person.

※ ※ ※

At the meeting attended by Mr. Fish and his companions, there were three kinds of talk:

(1) Talk in imitation of a backwater patois, from one speaker.
(2) Tough, simple talk, neutral in coloration, from a second speaker.
(3) New talk, based on the new relationship that is evolving between images and words, from a third speaker.

A discussion of the second kind of talk will reveal something about all three:

After the Second World War, there came into power at Harvard University, an old backwater near to the center of national life, a New Man. He was represented as having a point of view, but what he had in fact was a function and a tone of voice. His function was to make a new arrangement between the old backwater and national life. His tone of voice was neutral. This neutral tone of voice was his point of view. He was never asked to explain himself; his voice explained him. His effectiveness depended in some degree, however, on the presence at Harvard of certain old men, with whom he was juxtaposed. In the absence of these men, with whom he was in contrast, he looked very much like other strong, neutral men of his generation; that is, he seemed not particular but general. He had toughness and integrity. Here were two wirelike threads that linked him to his institution and to the old men who were his mentors. One decision he made demonstrated both his toughness and his integrity: he refused to adopt the manners of the old men, which were beguiling.

This man, where he continues to serve his institution, now represents the Old Guard of his institution. He is an important figure in that he does understand the ways of his backwater even though he has not adopted them himself. It must be difficult for him, in some cases, to welcome the newer sort of New Man, who knows the ways of the backwater very superficially and puts them on and casts them off as he pleases.

We may think of continuity within Harvard University as having three strands: toughness; manners; spirit. Wound together, they would have one destiny. They are not wound together; they are separate. After the Second World War, it was decided that toughness would continue into the next generation and manners would not. What of spirit?

It may be that the old men tried to pass on their spiritual inheritance to the new, tough man and failed. It may be that they did not try to pass on their spiritual inheritance. Or it may be, as it seems to me, that their spiritual inheritance had shrunk over time until it was no longer able to compete on equal terms with toughness or manners. It seems to me likely that by the time of the Second World War the spiritual inheritance of Harvard University was able to do very light work only; that the work it took on to do was to *enliven manners*; that it had become embedded *within* manners, so that when it was decided that manners would not continue, spirit (now known only as a form of energy within manners) died, too.

Not died — was not passed on. The spirit would not really die until the last self-confident old man died; and many self-confident old men lived on, more cheerful than ever.

※ ※ ※

What happened was that the work of running the university was separated from the work of maintaining its particular character. This explains the three kinds of talk. We have discussed the neutral tone of the second speaker. Now let us consider the two other kinds of talk.

A person attending Harvard after the Second World War might have decided to make a study of the inheritance of Harvard. In time, he would understand that his study was narrow; it was not, as he had thought, the study that embraced all the others. From that time, although his syntax would reflect his study of self-confidence, his reference would be to uncertainty. This was the first speaker.

Another person would find in the inheritance a kind of motif to be used to decorate, or to frame, whatever sort of *excellence* he wanted to promote. This was the third speaker, and also the film.

※ ※ ※

It will be the purpose of this essay to consider aspects of an inheritance; I will try to determine what it was that came to Harvard with the Black Rock Forest.

When I described Harvard as "an old backwater near to the center of national life," I was speaking of a former condition; Harvard is now a part of national life, and life there is not distinguishable from life anywhere else. When I used the phrase "old backwater near to the center of national life," there was nothing insulting in the use of the word "backwater;" I was thinking of the truck gardens that used to exist quite close to New York City and from which the city constantly drew refreshment.

❧ ❧ ❧

I would like to begin to introduce particular men into this story. My idea is that even the most difficult story ("Atomic Energy in the Modern World," "New Frontiers in Micro-Biology," "Our Colleges in Crisis") can be told as the history of the work of particular men and should be told that way.

The reader will accept this device. He is used to the idea that men, at their daily tasks, are occupying a certain space in the foreground. I want to address the question of the background against which these men appear, and to try to suggest that this background should be understood as the accumulated result of knowable stories.

This is important, because it is important to set right a deformation in modern discourse, a twofold mistake: the first part of the mistake is to think of the background against which the work of modern persons is juxtaposed as unknowable; the second part of the mistake is to accept it — whatever it is.

Now I want to introduce the idea of social embarrassment. One reason most people ignore — actually ignore — the question of the background against which their own lives are juxtaposed is that they imagine that some persons do understand this background (are in charge of it) and that these people-in-charge are their social betters. I would like to make the point in this regard that the President and Fellows of Harvard College and the college composed of living Harvard men and women do not understand the background against which modern lives are juxtaposed. It is only at fund-raising moments that they remember that they did, once, understand it.

🐾 🐾 🐾

A small beginning may be to tell the story of the Black Rock Forest in terms of the histories of particular men who were connected to it. Then places can be indicated at which this story may be said to join larger histories: of Harvard University, of the conservation policies of the government of the United States, of the history of optimistic thought within the conservation policies of the government, and of the history of science as it encloses the remarkable work done in physics and biology in this century.

🐾 🐾 🐾

First, a father.

James Stillman was a banker; he was thought by some people to be a ruthless one. He was associated with William Rockefeller, the brother of John D.

Rockefeller, and operated with Rockefeller and a small group of other men as a capitalist, which is to say that he was interested in the power of money within an enterprise, quite apart from any particular thing the enterprise was set up to do. The Stillman-Rockefeller group was described (by Henry Clews, a contemporary on Wall Street) as having resources so vast "that they need only concentrate on any given property in order to do with it what they please." As soon as this was known, they became unbearably attractive to investors. In the Amalgamated Copper manipulation, it was the reputation (for ruthlessness and vast resources) of the Rockefeller-Stillman manipulators that was attractive, more than the reputation of copper. The formula was, in some ways, the same as for older frenzies, like the South Sea Bubble, but the distant place where there was wealth beyond counting was in the Rockefeller-Stillman circle, as far as most investors were concerned, rather than in Montana.

🐿 🐿 🐿

Then a son.

Ernest Stillman, the youngest son of James Stillman, was a medical doctor. His impulse in all his activities seems to have been toward *healing*. He had an enthusiasm for firefighting, which seeks to remedy a spreading trouble. Also, we should note here that the land that was to constitute the Black Rock Forest was in a deplorable condition at the time Dr. Stillman inherited it from his father: these acres had been cut over for timber to be used (once reduced to charcoal) as fuel for the brickmaking factories along the Hudson. The land was the ruined remainder of the economic processes embraced and mastered by his father. Ernest Stillman wanted to bring this particular tract of land back to health, perhaps. More than that, he wanted to bring it back to health *for good*. His idea was that this protected forest, at least, should be constantly useful and also constantly flourishing.

🐜 🐜 🐜

Now I need to consider Gifford Pinchot, whose ideal the constantly useful, constantly flourishing forest was (he said that one of his goals for a forest was "sustained yield," and that the ideal against which conservation policies ought to be tested was "the greatest good of the greatest number for the longest time"), but first I want to mention one other man: Richard Thornton Fisher, of Harvard. Fisher was for many years (in the first half of this century) the head of the Harvard Forest, in Petersham, Massachusetts — a demonstration forest acquired in 1907. It was he who suggested to Dr. Ernest Stillman that the land he owned in the Hudson Highlands might be set up as a second demonstration forest. Richard Fisher seems to have acted in a fatherly way toward Dr. Stillman. Dr. Stillman's son Calvin Stillman has said that the death of Richard Fisher, in 1934, was the greatest blow Ernest Stillman suffered in his life. At Richard Fisher's death, a committee of Harvard alumni published a small book in his honor. The book was printed at the Cornwall Press, which was owned by Dr. Ernest Stillman. The book included this biographical note:

Richard T. Fisher entered Harvard with the Class of 1898, and in due time received his A.B. degree. He was an editor of the *Advocate* and a member of the O.K. Society and Hasty Pudding club. He specialized in courses in the English Department and graduated with honorable mention in English composition. Those of us who knew him as an undergraduate assumed that he was likely to devote himself to English studies and teaching. As a matter of fact, during the first winter after he graduated, he did serve the College as an assistant in Professor Wendell's and Professor Copeland's courses. But meanwhile an accidental combination of events determined his career. He spent the summer of '98 with a small party that C. Hart Merriam, then at the head of the U.S. Biological Survey, took out for a season of collecting on the upper slopes of Mount Shasta, and the experience with Merriam, more than any ordinary course in zoology, awoke in him a realization that what he most desired was some occupation that had to do with nature. Coincidentally, while on Mount Shasta, Fisher encountered Gifford Pinchot, who had just become Chief of the Division of Forestry (later developed into the United States Forest Service), and Mr. Pinchot offered him field work for the ensuing summer. Thereafter Fisher continued either in the Forest Service or on leave of absence as a student in the Yale Forest School, until he was appointed Instructor at Harvard. Before he began to teach he had thus been one of the enthusiastic and "closely knit group of men who helped Mr. Pinchot get the practice of forestry under way."

JAMES STILLMAN was one of a small number of men who discovered the life that money might have *as money*, apart from any particular work in the world — apart, even, from "rates of interest" and the ordinary terminology of the banker. He was one of a small number of men who saw that money might be *free*; that it might have a life of its own.

ERNEST STILLMAN, his youngest son, was drawn to *healing* work; he took particular interest in a particular tract of ravaged land, which he hoped to bring to health in such a way that it would stay useful and healthy for the longest time he could foresee.

RICHARD FISHER acted in a fatherly way to Ernest Stillman, and was embraced, perhaps, as a father by him. Richard Fisher had been, in his youth, "one of the enthusiastic and 'closely knit group of men who helped Mr. [Gifford] Pinchot get the practice of forestry under way.'"

❦ ❦ ❦

Gifford Pinchot was born on August 11, 1865, in Simsbury, Connecticut. His father had made a fortune in drygoods in New York City. His maternal grandfather, Amos Eno, was a successful investor in real estate and was the owner of the Fifth Avenue Hotel. Pinchot went to Exeter and Yale. Just before he enrolled at Yale, his father suggested to him that he make forestry his career. This was a most interesting intuition, since there was no forestry school at Yale, or anywhere in the country, at that moment. Pinchot wrote in his autobiography:

> So I took a course in meteorology, which has to do with weather and climate. And another in botany, which has to do with the vegetable kingdom — trees are unquestionably vegetable. And another in geology, for forests grow out of the earth. Also I took a course in astronomy, for it is the sun which makes trees grow.

He left America for Europe. When he returned, in 1890, he had studied the systematized forests of Europe. At that time, in America, the condition of the forests was very striking: vast forests had been thoroughly lumbered over and had been left in pitiable condition. Pinchot felt he had a role to play. His first work was for great magnates, however: he worked for W. Seward Webb in the Adirondacks and for Webb's connection George Washington Vanderbilt near Asheville, North Carolina.

🌲 🌲 🌲

The Vanderbilt family in America may be discussed in terms of the history of railroading, the history of social life, the history of architecture. In the history of architecture, they are secure in their place as promoters of gorgeous European styles. The family possessed almost a dozen large houses on Fifth Avenue in New York, the most remarkable of which was the "château" of Cornelius Vanderbilt III, at Fifty-seventh Street. Among their country houses were the house of Frederick Vanderbilt in Hyde Park, New York; the

Breakers and Marble House, at Newport; Florham, in New Jersey, the house of Hamilton Twombly and Florence Vanderbilt Twombly; and Biltmore, near Asheville, North Carolina, the house of George Washington Vanderbilt.

This last house has been known since the time of its building as "the largest private house in America." It was modelled on the château of Blois, but the work is not so finely done as it is at Blois. The interior is furnished with old European pieces and with imitations of such pieces. The house, which if it were in Europe would be beneath anyone's notice, is heavily visited by the public. The house is viewed by the public, I think, as a symbol of success, and it is that. It is representative of the failure of success to take hold in America. Some moment of success left this *thing*. People look at it, but they don't understand it.

Biltmore has shrunk. There was a forest; an arboretum was envisioned. What remains is the artifact-house. Frederick Law Olmsted was particularly interested in developing an arboretum at Biltmore. Gifford Pinchot (working as the "consulting forester" at Biltmore) wrote this enthusiastic prospectus, in 1893:

> It is the intention to make this Arboretum one of the finest in existence. There are already in the Nursery more kinds of trees and shrubs than there are in the Botanical Gardens at Kew, near London, and the number is being steadily increased. The climate will allow a larger variety of trees than that of any other large arboretum which has so far been

begun, while the liberal plan of the work is intended to make the best use of so admirable an opportunity. A careful record of the treatment of each species is being, and will be, kept; while a Forest Botanical Library, already of considerable extent, will furnish the necessary aid to study.

We may, for purposes of this essay, establish the *arboretum* as a symbol for one kind of activity undertaken in America with reference to a European model and *Biltmore House* as another. We see that the *arboretum* takes notice of the well-established gardens at Kew and means to outdo them — not as a result of an urgent interest in outdoing them but in consequence of certain natural advantages (here meteorological) to be found on this new continent. *Biltmore House*, on the other hand, has been built in an atmosphere of urgent need, and no natural advantages exist in North Carolina to support it. A third symbol is to be found in *Biltmore Forest.* The forest was that extensive portion of the Biltmore property given over to *scientific forest management.* It was described by Gifford Pinchot as follows:

> It is composed in greater part of Oaks and other deciduous trees, chiefly in the younger stages of their growth, with Pines scattered among the broad-leaved trees, and here and there pure patches of them in the old fields.

The forest, Pinchot said, "derives an additional interest from the fact that it is the first piece of woodland in the United States to be subjected to a regular system of management, the prime object of which is to pay the owner while improving the forest."

Of the condition of the forest at the time the "regular system of management" was instituted, Pinchot said,

> Previous to the time of purchase by Mr. George W. Vanderbilt, the area now included in Biltmore Estate was held by a number of small farmers. These people, poor as the mountain farmer is apt to be, were obliged to use without reserve all the resources of their scantily productive lands. They were therefore in the habit of cutting all trees which could be used or sold as fuel, fencing, or saw-logs. They turned their cattle into the forest, and often burned over their woodlands for the sake of the pasturage.... Under such treatment the forest, originally of moderate quality, grew steadily worse. The more valuable species of trees were removed, and the less valuable ones remained to seed the ground and perpetuate their kind. . . . At the time when forest management was begun on the Estate, the condition of a large part of the forest was deplorable in the extreme.

Pinchot did not stay long at Biltmore. In 1898, he went to work for the United States Department of Agriculture as the head of its Forestry Division. There he was called the Chief Forester; he was the first man to hold this version of the title, and it appealed to him, as he was the first American-born man to be a professional forester.

Pinchot's idea of what forestry might be can be thought of as having three parts. There was a scientific component, encompassing the study of the various factors that affect the growth and thrift of trees; a practical component, taking into consideration what goal was looked for in the culture and harvest of trees; and a conservative component, which sought to balance questions of usefulness in the short term and usefulness in the longer term. These three parts were not arcs of a circle but cups that fitted one inside another. The conservative part was the large cup into which scientific study and practical use were meant to fit.

There were objections to this point of view. To many men, Pinchot's arrangement seemed to use one cup too many. A simpler plan was to remove the scientific and the practical from the conservative-ethical context — to *free* them. We should take note of the opinions of two men who were at work in forestry at this time: Bernhard E. Fernow, who was Pinchot's predecessor at the Department of Agriculture; and Dr. Carl Alwin Schenck, a German forester, who succeeded Pinchot at Biltmore and was head of the Biltmore Forest School there.

Of methods of forestry which sought to assure a "sustained yield" over a long period, Fernow wrote in 1899:

> If then in a country [Germany] with dense population, where in many places every twig can be marketed, with settled conditions of market, with no virgin woods which could be cheaply exploited and come into advantageous competition with the

costlier material produced by managed properties, with cost of labor low and prices of wood comparatively high — if under such conditions the returns for the expenditure of money, skill, intellect in the production of wood crops [are] not more promising [returning from three to four per cent on invested capital], it would seem hopeless to develop the argument of profitableness in a country where all these conditions are the reverse, and a businessman considers a six per cent [return on] investment no sufficient inducement.

Of the Biltmore Forest School (which had been established in 1898 by Dr. Schenck and existed in one form or another until 1913), Dr. Schenck wrote, "I thought of it as a practical and technical school, the teachings of which, notably in lumbering and in financing, would be capable of immediate application in American woods."

We see that for Fernow and Schenck (as for later generations of lumbermen and graduates of forestry schools) the issue of forest management was not symbolic of some larger American issue. For Pinchot, it was. It is also true that his eye, more than the eyes of his contemporaries (Fernow and Schenck, for instance), was on the distant future. In America, the man who is reputed to be *forward-looking* wants only to see into the moment that is just beyond his grasp. The far distance has no interest for him. It may be the backward-looking man who thinks most clearly about the future. Pinchot wrote, in his book "The Fight for Conservation," in 1910:

Perhaps the most striking characteristic of the American people is their superb practical optimism; that marvellous hopefulness which keeps the individual efficiently at work. This hopefulness of the American is, however, as short-sighted as it is intense. As a rule, it does not look ahead beyond the next decade or score of years, and fails wholly to reckon with the real future of the Nation. I do not think I have often heard a forecast of the growth of our population that extended beyond a total of two hundred millions, and that only as a distant and shadowy goal. The point of view which this fact illustrates is neither true nor far-sighted. We shall reach a population of two hundred millions in the very near future, as time is counted in the lives of nations.

An enthusiastic man himself, he concerned himself with the question of what enthusiasm might do, and denied that it must inevitably apply itself to the stale job of increasing the momentum of whatever forces were already at work. He imagined, I think, that he had found an instant in time in which American enthusiasm might be redirected. His understanding of his country was unusual, and he was justified, perhaps, in thinking that he might shape it. He wrote:

No man may rightly fail to take a great pride in what has been accomplished by means of the destruction of our natural resources so far as it has gone. It is a paradoxical statement, perhaps, but nevertheless true, because out of this attack on what nature has given we have won a kind of prosperity and a kind of civilization and a kind of man that are new in the world. For example, nothing like the rapidity of the destruction of American forests has ever been known in forest history, and nothing like the efficiency and vigor and inventiveness of the American lumberman has ever been developed by any attack on any forests elsewhere. Probably the most effective tool that the human mind and hand have ever made is the American axe. So the American business man has grasped his opportunities and used them and developed them and invented about them, thought them into lines of success, and thus has developed into a new business man, with a vigor and effectiveness and a cutting-edge that have never been equalled anywhere else. We have gained out of the vast destruction of our natural resources a degree of vigor and power and efficiency of which every man of us ought to be proud.

Now that is done. We have accomplished these big things. What is the next step? Shall we go on in the same lines to the certain destruction of the prosperity which we have created, or shall we take the obvious lesson of all human history, turn our backs on the uncivilized point of view, and adopt toward our natural resources the average prudence and average foresight and average care that we long ago adopted as a rule of our daily life?

This is an unusual and interesting set of remarks. "We have gained out of the vast destruction of our natural resources a degree of vigor and power and efficiency of which every man of us ought to be proud." This is an unusual statement. An image comes to life here: a man on a piece of land. The land is damaged; the man has damaged it. But look: the man is powerful, strong, and happy. We recall that Frederick Law Olmsted saw a murderer (a man responsible for the death of many people) perform an act of high courage. This is what American history is like, but it is hard for us to accept: that a vigorous and splendid country could have been built by really guilty people. Nearly all statements in support of American enthusiasm describe only the nourishing power of enthusiasm, its ability to transform experience. Our attention is drawn, again and again, to the vigorous condition of the man with the axe. People who think that American enthusiasm ought to be curbed ignore this strong man and look only at the damage he has caused. Pinchot is one of a small number of powerful American men (Theodore Roosevelt and Franklin Roosevelt are others) who allow themselves to see *both* the glory of the vigorous man *and* the damage he has done. Pinchot takes note of the wonderful force that has been used to do the damage and asks that it be allowed to continue — but doing different work.

Men like Pinchot must ordinarily fail. Many Americans feel that it is in the contemplation of the possibility of uncontrolled recklessness that the nourishing power of enthusiasm actually resides; many other people have cultivated an interest in damage, and even in inventories of damaged things. Enthusiastic restraint is a difficult idea to grasp, and it is rarely put forward as a practical policy. But there were certain circumstances working in Pinchot's favor at the turn of the century. The forests of the country had been lumbered in such a reckless way that the result was obvious to the public. The near-total destruction of the pre-Colonial forest was as striking to people as the final depletion of American oil reserves will be. Moreover, Pinchot found that he had the ear of Theodore Roosevelt, who was unexpectedly elevated to the Presidency by the assassination of William McKinley in 1901.

❧ ❧ ❧

In 1926, Richard Thornton Fisher, the director of the Harvard Forest, in Petersham, Massachusetts, walked over a tract of land in Cornwall, New York, owned by his friend Dr. Ernest Stillman. Like the land that had been formed into the Biltmore Estate, this was damaged land that had been purchased from many small-holders by a rich man — in this case, Dr. Stillman's father, the banker James Stillman. Richard Fisher urged Dr. Stillman to establish this tract as a demonstration forest. It was so established, and was called the Black Rock Forest; the name derived from Black Rock Mountain, one of a number of high hills within the tract. A system of publications (Bulletins and Papers) describing the work being done within the forest was established as well.

Richard Fisher contributed an introduction to the first Black Rock Forest Bulletin, in 1930. He wrote:

The Black Rock Forest, from which this bulletin is the first publication, is probably the first institution of its kind to be established in the United States — a private property organized as a forest laboratory for research in problems of forest management and for the demonstration of successful methods in practice. In carrying out this purpose, for which a great deal of the preliminary work is already done, the Forest has every prospect of rendering a valuable public service. The tract is of ample size, and by reason of its location and good protective organization it is relatively safe from fire. Adequate financing and expert supervision assure it of efficient management. Moreover, the Black Rock Forest represents a region where the problem of the future use of land is of peculiar economic and social importance, and where but little systematic work has been done to solve it.

In the hills of northern New Jersey and the Highlands of the Hudson, almost at the back doors of the greatest center of population in the country, there is in the aggregate a very large area of rough, wooded land, much of it still practically a wilderness. For generations it has been repeatedly cut over for wood and many times ravaged by fire. As a result many of the better species of trees have become scarce, inferior kinds have increased growth and reproductive capacity is enfeebled, and the soil is impoverished. For most of this type of land — rocky, steep, and thin-soiled — the only foreseeable use is for recreation or forest products. For either purpose economy requires that the forest should be rejuvenated in growth and value and the soil restored as far as possible to its maximum fertility. To this end it is necessary that the right methods be worked out to eliminate the worthless and to increase the growth and reproduction of the better species, to restore the fertility of the soil, and in time to define the types of vegetation that will make the best use of these rough and stony sites.

It is the program of the Black Rock Forest to supply this needed knowledge, not only by publishing periodically the results of experimental work, but by displaying to visitors the various areas or plots in the woods where different kinds of treatment have been applied and how they have succeeded. Looking to the future relation between the metropolitan area and its nearest available region of wild land, this will be a service of the greatest value.

When Richard Fisher wrote the introduction to the first Bulletin, he was fifty-four. Thirty-seven years had passed since Gifford Pinchot issued his description of the work to be undertaken within Biltmore Forest. Thirty-two years had passed since Fisher encountered Gifford Pinchot on Mount Shasta.

We might return for a moment to Pinchot's description of the work he was doing (and planned to do) at Biltmore. This description is contained in a booklet entitled "Biltmore Forest," which was written in connection with an exhibit taken by the Biltmore Estate to the Columbian Exposition of 1893. The following quotation is from "Planting," a section in which Pinchot laid out his plans for planting trees in certain patches of wasteland at Biltmore:

> The plan upon which the forest planting is to be undertaken is a wide one and is likely to produce important results. We are acquainted with a great number of exotic species in their garden character: we know very few of them as to their adaptation to Forest uses. Of the silvicultural character of American trees we are almost equally ignorant. It is intended, therefore, to plant blocks of an acre or more of each of a very large number of American and foreign trees, assigning each to the character of land which it is most likely to occupy with advantage. . . . Such an experiment may be expected, in the course of time, to add many important species to the useful forest flora of the country.

This quotation introduces the idea of planting trees, which Pinchot did not in general favor; he preferred to concern himself with natural reproduction within the forest. And it contains the interesting remark "Of the silvicultural character of American trees we are almost equally ignorant."

This is a true statement to this day, and it is clear why: it is hard to get to know the silvicultural character of trees (there are countless elements that affect the growth of trees in situ over their long life), and, given the way we prefer to live in America, there is no very good reason for trying. The situation might be compared with one in which people neglect to pay attention to the specific things that make one particular town healthy, because these specific things are very complex and hard to pin down, because mastery of these things promises success only in one particular place, and because people have become habituated to towns of standardized manufacture. We know about trees what we think we need to know, and what is *exciting* to know. That is, we know what men at work in basic science tell us is true for *very many trees* or *all trees*; we know from experience which species, growing under what conditions, harvested in which way, fit best into the framework of our economic life as it exists now. Nearly all else is still hidden.

We might return again to the symbols within the Biltmore Estate. *Biltmore House* represents an attempt to establish a place within national life. It is *everywhere and nowhere*. It has little to do with North Carolina. The *arboretum* has roots in the specific conditions to be found near Asheville, North Carolina, but with reference to other arboretums, elsewhere. Within the *forest* there is a promise of information that may, over time, be found to be useful in other places, but first of all it is what it is: a forest in North Carolina, tending to good health or poor.

Everywhere and nowhere is the way of national life and is also the place where *basic scientific research* is to be found. It may be of interest to some few persons that the first work was done in this or that place, but the success of the work is in proportion to the degree to which the work is diffused throughout the world.

Here and there is the manner of the museum, where the location of the collection is only part of the issue.

Mostly here is the way of silviculture, and also of human settlements, which must necessarily be affected by specific local conditions.

In recent times, the first two ways of being in a place have been much more important to the American people than the third — this despite the fact that everyone does live in some particular place. As a result, very little is known about how this or that particular place might be brought into a healthy condition.

☙ ☙ ☙

In 1940, Dr. Ernest Stillman wrote a letter to Dr. James B. Conant, the president of Harvard University, and enclosed a memorandum he had written on the subject of the Harvard Forest and the Black Rock Forest. Dr. Stillman urged Harvard to give a greater attention to the Harvard Forest, which he felt was being neglected. He also urged Harvard to agree to accept the Black Rock Forest at his death. I do not know exactly what position Harvard was taking at this time about the Harvard Forest (of which Dr. Stillman was the principal benefactor) and the Black Rock Forest (of which Dr. Stillman was the sole proprietor); the relevant documents are protected by a "fifty-year rule" — under which documents are withheld from public scrutiny for fifty years. The university seems to have been reluctant to commit itself to taking on the Black Rock Forest. "As long as the late Professor Fisher approved . . . the idea of Black Rock Forest becoming a part of the forestry plant of the University, naturally I erroneously assumed that the necessary arrangements had been made," Dr. Stillman wrote in 1940 in his letter to Conant. Apparently, the necessary arrangements had not been made.

In the memorandum that accompanied his letter to President Conant, Dr. Stillman discussed several plans (to be financed in large part by Dr. Stillman himself) that he felt would bring the Harvard Forest into greater prominence. He referred to the Harvard Forest as "a barely explored academic gold mine." He advanced the opinion that a set of forest models, financed by him, would interest not only distinguished visitors but also the general public. He wrote that "the members of the biological staffs have not made use of [the forest's] resources because of lack of proper housing facilities." To that sentence Professor Hugh Raup, of the Arnold Arboretum, at Harvard, appended this note:

> This isn't the only reason. Most of the biological staff at Harvard is uninterested as yet in the things they can find at Petersham. *It is hard to control experiments outside of the laboratory*; hence, the dyed-in-the-wool laboratory man is often afraid to work "in the open field." [Raup's emphasis.]

Of the Black Rock Forest property Dr. Stillman wrote:

> The Black Rock Forest in its 12 years of life has already produced so much valuable scientific knowledge that it seemed a shame to have these

experiments terminate at my death. Three alternatives presented themselves: (1) establish an individual foundation; (2) deed the property to the Bronx Botanical Park, Syracuse or Cornell Universities; or (3) deed the property to Harvard University.

I discarded the first, as the management would be too narrow. I naturally favored the last, as I believe the Black Rock Forest would be complementary to the Harvard Forest. In order that the Forest would not be a burden on the University, I arranged to set up an endowment, the income of which could be used to defray the expenses of operating both the Black Rock Forest and the Harvard Forest. If the corporation decides not to accept the Black Rock Forest with its endowment, I must make other arrangements.

Harvard accepted the gift. I imagine this conversation:

FELLOW OF HARVARD: And then there is the
    question of the Black Rock Forest.
PRESIDENT OF HARVARD: Not again!
FELLOW: I think we ought to accept it, you know.
PRESIDENT: Why? We already have a forest and I'm
    not aware we need another.
FELLOW: One must distinguish between spinsters.
    The Forest we have and will continue to have
    (for no one will allow us to part from her) is
    poor; at best, she just gets by, and (there is no
    end to our bad luck) her most faithful friend has

been the gentleman who wants to give us Forest
No. 2.

PRESIDENT: No one knows what we suffer from the
generosity of our graduates!

FELLOW: There must be special rewards for those
who suffer in silence.

PRESIDENT: I approve of silence.

FELLOW: The temple.

PRESIDENT: The *grave*. And Forest No. 2 is . . .

FELLOW: Rich.

PRESIDENT: And unselfish! I know this old maid.
She does not spend money on herself! Brave in
adversity, she shrinks from her own large
income; it's the one thing she dreads. Dividends
and interest are anathema to her, and yet she
must spend, lest her enormous capital grow more
grotesquely huge, producing an income even
more unwieldy. Without a poor relation on
whom to lavish care she is— . . . lost! A
nightmare dilemma. I see our duty now.

FELLOW: Once again, you have pierced to the heart
of the matter. And who knows? In time . . .

PRESIDENT: She may wander off. What's the name?

FELLOW: Black Rock Forest.

PRESIDENT: Or find a beau who doesn't like
dowries.

FELLOW: That man is rare.

PRESIDENT: She'd only want the special case.

THE FOREST

Soon after the Harvard fund-raising event at the United States Military Academy, I went to see Mr. Esty Stowell. Mr. Stowell is a graduate of Harvard College, Class of 1934. He maintains a house in Cornwall, New York, near the Black Rock Forest. He said, "We have known for some time that Harvard had lost interest in the forest. John Stillman, a son of Dr. Stillman's, who lives here, wrote to Harvard sometime in the nineteen-fifties, and someone there wrote back saying, Oh, we are doing this and that. But nothing has really gone on in the forest for years and years — although Harvard does keep the roads up. In any case, after the Storm King issue came up — in the early nineteen-sixties, if you remember, Con Edison wanted to build a pumped-storage plant here — Harvard appointed a committee to see what its response should be to Con Edison's proposal, because some acres of the forest would have been taken. Somewhere in the report of that committee, it says that Harvard should think about getting rid of the forest, because no real work was being done in it. Rather like the railroads, you see. It runs down, and then people say, 'Impossible to go on, it's so run down.' In any case, some few of us went on the alert after that. Over the whole period, Harvard has been very elusive. There was a period in the middle seventies when it pursued a deal with the Palisades Interstate Park Commission, but the Park Commission was not able after all to get the funds it would have needed to buy the forest, so that fell through.

And then, you see, we began to worry that Harvard, having begun this process, might consider *any buyer*, and a few of us began to ask, and ask again, what Harvard's intentions were. I began a correspondence with Daniel Steiner, Harvard's general counsel, and what I got back in most instances was a total mouthful of feathers. 'No decision has been reached; we're not talking to anyone at this moment.' It was 'Harvard will do the right thing' kind of talk. He won't say much except that Harvard feels secure in its legal position, because Dr. Stillman did not put any language in his will saying that the forest must revert to his heirs if Harvard didn't follow a given course of action. That's what makes John Stillman so angry: he says — quite rightly, I think — that of course his father didn't use that language, because he trusted Harvard. Besides, you know, I think Harvard doesn't like accepting gifts with that kind of restriction, and it probably asked him to make the bequest as simple as possible, but that's a guess.

"There are so many issues here. First of all, the forest is very interesting, you know. It was set up to look into various practical problems: woodlot management and so forth — just the sort of thing people are interested in now. Wouldn't you think Harvard would think about that? Well, it doesn't. And, of course, the forest is beautiful. My wife and I walk in it all the time; the roads and trails are marvellous. We have been just about everywhere, I would say, except down to Glycerine Hollow. It's all terribly well done. I mean, it has been laid out with care, and, of course, there are experimental plots all through it, testing whether this sort of tree grows best here or there. I wish I could tell you more about that, but I can't. You would have liked Henry Tryon, who was the forester here. He was what I call a rough diamond. Always wore red suspenders. His attitude toward the forest was almost the attitude of a poet. There was a sign that Hal Tryon had erected which no longer stands. It was a yard square, I would say. And on it — very neat — was a description of a cycle in silviculture. And it concluded with this: 'The trees were cut; their work was done.' There was an amateur poet shining through. He had that spirit — an *amateur*, in the old sense. He was a big, burly, red-haired Harvard guy. Ex-football player.

"I would say the important issue is: Harvard gave its word.

"You must walk around the forest. It's laid out so well; you can take short walks or quite long ones. We'll go on a short one today. On another day, I suggest you make a circuit. I will give you a map. You might go south as far as Spy Rock and Eagle Cliff. That's a good day's walk.

"And go and talk to Steiner. We can't get much out of him. Just that Harvard feels secure in its legal position."

If a person were to walk through the Black Rock Forest today, starting from the entrance to the forest, at the Upper Reservoir, he might climb the Hill of Pines to the top, where there is a fine view all around. He might look at pitch pine and scrub oak (Henry Tryon assumed that they constituted one of the few scraps of the pre-Colonial pattern remaining within the Forest), then descend to Carpenter Road (an ample, well-maintained dirt road), head west on Carpenter Road, then southwest on Bog Meadow Road to the white-blazed trail called the Scenic Trail, then walk on the Scenic Trail to Eagle Cliff, elevation 1,443 feet. This is about as far south as a person can go in the forest. From this spot, there is a wonderful view south in the direction of New York City. It is the sort of view that no one thinks can exist close to New York City — the sort of thing that a person heads west for. From here, a route back to the entrance to the forest might be: the Scenic Trail again until the turnoff to the Chatfield Trail; the Chatfield Trail to Chatfield Road; east on Chatfield Road to the White Oak Trail, passing the Tamarack Pond and the Chatfield farmhouse (a splendid stone building of 1834), and passing a tract reforested in red pine by Henry Tryon; west on the White Oak Trail to Sutherland Road; northeast on Sutherland Road to the Schunemunk — Storm King Trail; up Black Rock, elevation 1,410; down to the Aleck Meadow Reservoir and White Oak Road. This would take most of one day.

On another day, a person might go to Glycerine Hollow. This would be a short trip: south from the entrance to the forest to Carpenter Road by the Hill of Pines Trail and then to Go-Down Road. No route could be finer than Go-Down Road. It is broader than a trail but narrower now than a road. It is a road gone gentle. It is grassy most of its length and descends at a good rate. It does not twist and turn. It goes straight to where it is going.

This is what Henry Tryon said in 1939 in his Ten Year Progress Report about Glycerine Hollow and his work there:

Nine and one-half acres of mixed hardwood association, about seventy years old, were marked for cleaning in the autumn of 1928. Our original plan was to follow this operation with two, or perhaps more, improvement cuttings with the object of encouraging reproduction of the better commercial species. The original stand was (and still is) about the best timber in the Forest. Form and height are unusually good.

But advance growth was hard to find. Our cleaning operation, which removed the dead, dying, overtopped and deformed stems, with an occasional intermediate or codominant, tallied, to our great surprise, 16.8 cords per acre. The appearance of the area was at first unusually clean and neat, but the inevitable sprout growth soon altered this.

Here as in Cutting 1d, nothing appeared at first but sprouts. By 1934, however, a setting of young white ash, red oak, sugar maple, and yellow poplar was showing. The density of this new growth made us wonder if our projected additional cuttings would be needed. By 1936 the reproduction of these species was so numerous that we abandoned entirely our idea of extra cuttings and decided to leave matters temporarily as they were.

This stand can be left to grow for at least fifty years longer. It is a crop of medium-sized, valuable sawlogs now, with easy accessibility. The additional volume increment will raise the money return from the final cutting; the overwood appears to be in excellent health, with no danger of decadence for a long period, and the reproduction is becoming well established. A final cutting could be made tomorrow; but we see no merit in that. We believe the best plan will be to delay harvesting this area until a strongly favorable market becomes available. It is interesting to note that the thinning applied here in 1928–29, while apparently heavy on a volume basis, did not admit sufficient light to stimulate water-sprouting to any marked extent.

Here, too, future investigation may reveal that our "tinkering" with the species association of this particular site has caused an upset. Conversely, we may perhaps find that our slight rearrangement of the composition (for here we expect to increase but slightly the percentage of white ash and yellow poplar) is precisely what nature has been seeking to accomplish. In contrast with Cutting 1a, the anticipated composition will not differ as sharply from the old mixture. Cutting 2a is another test plot in our search to determine what species mixture will give the highest yield on this particular site. We may learn that we are wide of the mark or perhaps we shall be agreeably surprised.

Much important information is implicit in these paragraphs. Notice all the room for judgment: not now, later; this much, no more. Notice the room for the adjustment of judgment: we may be wrong, of course. And the acknowledgment of the possibility of grace: we may be in for a pleasant surprise. Notice these recorded facts:

(1) The forest is not a magnificent stand of virgin timber. It is a magnificent place, with a history of abuse. In the whole of the forest, Glycerine Hollow has the best stand of timber, and in 1928 that was merely seventy years old.

(2) The timber is meant to be harvested in the end, as part of the natural rhythm of the work of men. There is a trust in the possibilities of work. A man who had come to distrust the work of men might have said, "See here, this is good. Let's at least keep our hands off this." A devilish man who had come to despise the work of men might have said, "This is good. What of it?" Tryon's opinion is one never heard in our day: "This is good. Let us put our good hands on it."

CHRONOLOGIES

In July, 1898, James Wilson, Secretary of Agriculture to President McKinley, appointed Gifford Pinchot to be Chief Forester of the United States in the Department of Agriculture. Here Pinchot had a tiny staff, and no forests to manage, because the forest reserves superintended by the federal government were under the jurisdiction of the Secretary of the Interior. In the absence of federal land to look into, Pinchot turned to questions relating to the management of private land. On October 15, 1898, his division issued Circular 21, which announced a management-assistance program for large tracts of timberland and small woodlots. Small owners could apply for free assistance; large holders of land were expected to share the cost. Numbers of landholders, small and large, sought help. The expansion of his work load justified the expansion of his operation, and in 1899 Pinchot reported, "The Division has been thoroughly equipped with instruments for field work, in which it was wholly lacking at the beginning of the year." It was also drawing to it the services of enthusiastic men, many of them recent college graduates, who worked for little money and came to be known as "Pinchot's young men." And the liveliness of this operation, in turn, generated more work, and inquiries from the Department of the Interior.

Then Theodore Roosevelt became President of the United States. While he was governor of New York State, he had consulted with Pinchot. "Like other men who had thought about the national future at all, I had been growing more and more concerned over the destruction of the forests," Roosevelt wrote in his "Autobiography." When Roosevelt came to Washington after the assassination of President McKinley, he did not go immediately to the White House but stopped at the house of a sister. Gifford Pinchot and his colleague Frederick H. Newell came to call on him there. "The first work I took up when I became President was the work of reclamation," Roosevelt wrote.

It might be well to describe here Roosevelt's attitude toward conservation. It was influenced by Pinchot, but it was in keeping with other beliefs of his. *Proper use* might describe it. His faith in himself was abundant, and also his faith in the idea of individual persons making judgments. He was apt to endorse Pinchot's idea of silviculture, since he took the view that the nation itself was like a forest, in which *good thrift* and healthy reproduction could be encouraged. A striking and, to modern minds, an extreme instance of his belief in distinction-making is to be found in his attitude toward large business combinations. He wrote:

> Where a company is found seeking its profits through serving the community by stimulating production, lowering prices or improving service, while scrupulously respecting the rights of others (including its rivals, its employees, its customers, and the general public), and strictly obeying the law, then no matter how large its capital, or how great the volume of its business, it would be encouraged to still more abundant production.

As we discuss the inheritance present within the Black Rock Forest, in Cornwall, New York, this quality of optimism should be remembered, and distinguished from the idea, now coming to prevail in America, that impersonal forces rule the world, and that clever men ally themselves with these forces, while idealistic men struggle to move certain valued things out of their way.

In 1905, the forest lands managed by the Interior Department were transferred to the Department of Agriculture, where Gifford Pinchot was Chief Forester. In 1907, more than forty-three million acres of land were added by Presidential proclamation to the area of the National Forests. "By this time, also," Roosevelt wrote in his "Autobiography," "the opposition of the servants of the special interests in Congress to the Forest Service had become strongly developed, and more time appeared to be spent in the yearly attacks upon it during the passage of the appropriation bills than on all other Government Bureaus put together. Every year the Forest Service had to fight for its life."

He continued:

One incident in these attacks is worth recording. While the Agricultural Appropriation Bill was passing through the Senate, in 1907, Senator Fulton, of Oregon, secured an amendment providing that the President could not set aside any additional National Forests in the six Northwestern States. This meant retaining some sixteen million of acres to be exploited by land grabbers and by the representatives of the great special interests, at the expense of the public interest. But for four years the Forest Service had been gathering field notes as to what forests ought to be set aside in these States, and so was prepared to act. It was equally undesirable to veto the whole agricultural bill, and to sign it with this amendment effective. Accordingly, a plan to create the necessary

National Forest in these States before the Agricultural Bill could be passed and signed was laid before me by Mr. Pinchot. I approved it. The necessary papers were immediately prepared. I signed the last proclamation a couple of days before, by my signature, the bill became law; and when the friends of the special interests in the Senate got their amendment through and woke up, they discovered that sixteen million acres of timberland had been saved for the people by putting them in the National Forests before the land grabbers could get at them. The opponents of the Forest Service turned handsprings in their wrath; and dire were their threats against the Executive; but the threats could not be carried out, and were really only a tribute to the efficiency of our action.

The ethic of restraint put forward by Pinchot and Roosevelt proved to be too small a vessel to hold the enthusiastic ambition of many independent men, who called it "Pinchotism." Nonetheless, during Theodore Roosevelt's Administration the area of the National Forests increased from forty-three million acres to a hundred and ninety-four million.

By the end of Roosevelt's time in office, Pinchot and Roosevelt had begun to think of conservation as a worldwide movement. A North American Conservation Conference was held at the White House on February 18, 1909. "It is evident that natural resources are not limited by the boundary lines which separate nations," Roosevelt wrote in his invitation (delivered in person by Gifford Pinchot) to the Prime Minister of Canada and the President of Mexico. The North American Conservation Conference met for five days and, in its communiqué to Roosevelt, suggested that "all nations should be invited to join together in conference on the subject of world resources, and their inventory, conservation, and wise utilization." Soon afterward, Roosevelt left office. The worldwide conservation conference envisioned by Pinchot and Roosevelt did not take place.

Pinchot was removed from office by Roosevelt's successor, William Howard Taft — a fact that Roosevelt noted bitterly in his "Autobiography." "Gifford Pinchot is the man to whom the nation owes most for what has been accomplished as regards the preservation of the natural resources of our country," he wrote. "I believe it is but just to say that among the many, many public officials who under my administration rendered literally invaluable service to the people of the United States, he, on the whole, stood first."

In looking again at the phrase "what has been accomplished as regards the preservation of the natural resources of our country," we must admit that while Pinchot had succeeded in bringing a vast amount of land under public stewardship he had not succeeded in bringing his idea of conservation into a synthesis with the national enthusiasm for work. Pinchot has described a moment early in a December, 1908, governors' meeting when he began to understand what President-elect Taft's position would be:

The first words Taft spoke after I called the meeting to order and introduced him as its presiding officer gave us the clue. He said:

"Mr. President, Ladies and Gentlemen: There is one difficulty about the conservation of natural resources. It is that the imagination of those who are pressing it may outrun the practical facts."

LETTER OF MARCH 2, 1909

Dear Gifford:

I have written you about others; I have written you about many public matters; now, just a line about yourself. As long as I live I shall feel for you a mixture of respect and admiration and of affectionate regard. I am a better man for having known you. I feel that to have been with you will make my children better men and women in after life; and I cannot think of a man in the country whose loss would be a more real misfortune to the Nation than yours would be. For seven and a half years we have worked together, and now and then played together — and have been altogether better able to work because we have played; and I owe to you a peculiar debt of obligation for a very large part of the achievement of this Administration.

With love to your dear mother, I am,

Ever faithfully your friend,

Theodore Roosevelt

OTHER LETTERS OF 1909
Theodore Roosevelt, on the 'Nzor River,
to his daughter Ethel:
Darling Ethel:

Here we are, by a real tropical river, with game all around, and no human being within several days' journey. At night the hyenas come round the camp, uttering their queer howls; and once or twice we have heard lions; but unfortunately have never seen them. Kermit killed a leopard yesterday. He has really done so very well! It is rare for a boy with his refined tastes and his genuine appreciation of literature — and of so much else — to be also an exceptionally bold and hardy sportsman. He is still altogether too reckless; but by my hen-with-one-chicken attitude, I think I shall get him out of Africa uninjured; and his keenness, cool nerve, horsemanship, hardihood, endurance, and good eyesight make him a really good wilderness hunter. We have become genuinely attached to Cunninghame and Tarleton, and all three naturalists, especially Heller; and also to our funny black attendants. The porters always amuse us; at this moment about thirty of them are bringing in the wood for the camp fires, which burn all night; and they are all chanting in chorus, the chant being nothing but the words "*Wood* — plenty of wood to burn!"

A Merry Christmas to you! And to Archie and Quentin. How I wish I were to be with you all, no matter how cold it might be at Sagamore; but I suppose we shall be sweltering under mosquito nets in Uganda.

Edward H. Harriman, from Aiken,
South Carolina, to James Stillman, in Cannes:
Dear Stillman:

I've been idling here with the idlers for a week and am in normal condition again. I really had a nasty breakdown just before Christmas, apparently poisoned by something eaten at one of the big functions. It got completely into my system. Dr. Delafield nursed me back to life and I'm now O.K. again. We leave for Savannah today, thence to Atlanta and Macon, Augusta and North by Thursday next. Bertie Goelet came with me and we stayed with Joe Harriman, his wife being in New York. My girls all in midst of New York engagements and fine, and I couldn't bring any of them away.

Taft has been at Augusta all winter and left yesterday for Charleston, remains till tomorrow and then sails away for Panama. This latter trip many of us think should not be taken. All I can hear from close by indicates that the next Administration will be dignified, fair as well as progressive — the outlook from that quarter is good. Business conditions are certainly conservative which is also good. Our people are getting used to having money on hand without considering it necessary to speculate with it. I had a short talk with John D. R. yesterday and expect to see him again in a few days, he seemed in satisfied frame of mind. I'll make it short though. I want to get back home and prepare for a long trip South and West in February and March. Wish you were here to go. I am sorry indeed about your daughter and hope she may find something and somewhere that will help her to restored health. I sympathize with your feeling regarding her. The Poniatowskis have written about Christmas — thank you for doing this for me.

Sincerely yours,

E.H.H.

James Stillman, from Cannes,
to his mother, in America:

My dear Mother:

I am so sorry to hear you have had a cold, but was greatly relieved to learn from a cablegram received yesterday that you were able to go out of doors again. Still the coming two months are the most trying ones in our treacherous climate and you must be most careful. Elsie and I are delighted to receive letters from you, but pray don't tire yourself by writing. She is, I am so glad to be able to say, much better. Cannes has done her much good. I am so sorry we cannot remain longer, as we are obliged to leave for Paris tomorrow so she can prepare for the presentation at court. I return with fear and trembling on her account to the damp and chilly climate of Paris and especially that of London at this season of the year, but both she and I have been determined to be presented. I hope the fatigue and excitement will do her no harm, if not, the brilliant function will be a pleasant recollection. We may return here again if it is not thought best for her to go home in March, but we are all beginning to be quite anxious to return, and it will be such a very great pleasure to see you again. I sent Bessie the other day an Italian Railroad folder filled with illustrations. I hope they will interest her, they did me.

Last evening we had such a gorgeous red and pink sunset and this evening a yellow one.

I have never seen anything like them before, and the wonderful coloring of the land, water and sky continually changing at the different times of the day. Then the beautiful flowers and trees. I never see them without thinking of how you would enjoy them. What do you say to our renting a villa here for next winter, when you could be out of doors every day? I think it would be most enjoyable. We will talk it over when I return, which I hope now will be soon. With much love to everyone, I am

Your affectionate son,
James Stillman

James Stillman, from London, to his mother:
My dear Mother:
Your lovely letter of the Eleventh instant has just been forwarded to me here from Paris. I appreciate it very deeply and have given it to Elsie to read. Soon the bright spring days will be here, and I hope we can all be together again in Cornwall this summer. We are here for the Court ceremonies and after they are over will probably return to the Riviera for a month before going home, most likely at the same hotel in Cannes from which the view is most beautiful.

Elsie and I have just returned from making our obeisance before the august presence of His Imperial Majesty at St. James's Palace. It was a very brilliant spectacle. Diplomats and the Military in gorgeous uniforms, Bishops in their robes of all colors, judges with their wigs and gowns, and although our court costume (which was velvet and knee breeches covered with silver buttons and buckles, cocked hat and sword, which we were afraid would trip us) was very fine, we were quite modest in comparison.

Friday we go to the great Court at Buckingham Palace with Elsie and her gown with a train nearly four yards long. It is very beautiful and becoming to her. Worth, who made it, I can see realizes he has made a success, although he never made anything like the train before. The gown is soft white satin with silver embroidery, the train is a sort of mosquito netting with whole brilliants sown on it about an inch apart, laid on a rather stiff, dull silvery material lined with a soft white satin with a border of Russian sable all around it, which shows the lines and serves as a frame setting it off beautifully. It's really very magnificent but still youthful and appropriate for her. You must not think we are too worldly. The object of interesting her, the preparation, the meeting of people, the attention shown, is better and more effective than medicine and has done her lots of good — which will please you if my description of the gown does not. With love to you all, I am

Your affectionate son,
James S.

Robert W. Sayles, assistant in charge of
the geological collection at the Museum of
Comparative Zoology, in Cambridge, to
Jerome D. Greene, Secretary to the Corporation,
Harvard University:

My dear Mr. Greene:

A little while ago Mr. Ernest G. Stillman, the son of James Stillman, gave me a collection of Japanese lantern slides, the pictures of which he took himself. He intends that they shall go to the Department of Geology and Geography. They are now in the Gardner Collection, but the gift [is] to the Department of Geology and Geography. Mr. Stillman's address is #9 East 72nd Street, New York City.

Yours very truly,

Robert W. Sayles

❦ ❦ ❦

We are now in a position, perhaps, to put down a chronology:

(1) In 1893, Gifford Pinchot, twenty-eight years old, prepared a booklet that described the work he was undertaking and planned to undertake near Asheville, North Carolina, at Biltmore Forest — a tract of land owned by George Washington Vanderbilt, who was engaged also in the building of a large country house, Biltmore, modelled in large part on the château of Blois.

(2) In July, 1898, James Wilson, Secretary of Agriculture under President McKinley, appointed Pinchot to be Chief Forester in the Department of

Agriculture. Pinchot had a tiny staff and no forests to manage.

(3) In the summer of 1898, Pinchot encountered Richard Thornton Fisher, who had just graduated from Harvard College, on Mount Shasta, in California. Pinchot offered Fisher a job for the next summer, and Fisher became one of the "closely knit group of men who helped Mr. Pinchot get the practice of forestry under way."

(4) On September 14, 1901, President McKinley died from wounds suffered from an assassin's bullets, and Theodore Roosevelt assumed the Presidency. When Roosevelt arrived in Washington, he went to the house of a sister. Pinchot and his colleague Frederick Newell called on him there. Pinchot was then thirty-six years old. Theodore Roosevelt later wrote, "The first work I took up when I became President was the work of reclamation." By "reclamation" he meant in particular forest work and the irrigation of arid lands. In general, he meant a policy that would encourage the *proper use* of all the nation's natural resources.

(5) In 1909, Theodore Roosevelt left office. Gifford Pinchot was dismissed by President Taft the following year.

※ ※ ※

In any event, the chronology is a short one. If we put the beginning at 1892, when Pinchot began his work at Biltmore, the first native-born American trained to be a forester, it encompasses less than twenty years. It must end at 1909. More than twenty years passed before the government took an active role in conservation again, and then it was an obvious catastrophe that gave rise to action: the "dust bowl," in the plains region. In this case, soil and agriculture were the focus of action. There was among some people an interest in finding a generative symbol in the government's attempt to conserve the soil, but soon the ethical aspect of soil conservation was forgotten, while the practical lessons were reduced to simple formulas related to immediate yield. The conservation movement of our own day has little to do with either the soil-conserving activity of the nineteen-thirties or the conservative-forestry ethic of the turn of the century. The modern conservationist must attempt to modify pathological symptoms unimagined by the men we have been discussing; or he will see to *preserve* this or that piece of nature by getting it out of the way of the world's work. He is, typically, either a scientist experienced in toxicology or a lawyer — not a farmer or a forester.

Pinchot's idea of conservative forestry, we have said, resembled a nest of cups: practicality and science resting one within the other, and both resting within a conservative ethic that he articulated as "the greatest good of the greatest number for the longest time" — a dictum he later attributed to William J. McGee, an ethnologist he described as "the scientific brains of the Conservation Movement." This ethic had no consistent advocate within the federal government after 1909, but it did continue to hold the interest of certain men, whose history we are able to trace. Here is a minor chronology (to append to the important one above), which will lead us to the Black Rock Forest:

(1) In 1898, Richard Thornton Fisher met Gifford Pinchot on Mount Shasta and became one of "the closely knit group of men who helped Mr. Pinchot get the practice of forestry under way."

(2) In 1926, Richard Thornton Fisher walked over a tract of land in Cornwall, New York, with Dr. Ernest Stillman, a son of James Stillman, and urged him to establish a demonstration forest on it.

(3) In 1928, the Black Rock Forest was established by Dr. Ernest Stillman.

(4) In 1949, the Black Rock Forest came, with a generous endowment, into the possession of the President and Fellows of Harvard College.

Now we may describe some important aspects of the inheritance that Harvard received when the Black Rock Forest came into its possession:

(1) The ability to do, within the forest, scientific work that had the potential of wide application. For instance, Professor Hugh Raup, of the Arnold Arboretum, wrote (at the time when Dr. Stillman was approaching Harvard on the subject of the forest):

One of the most important features of the Black Rock Forest as a prospective part of the Harvard Forest organization is that it would materially broaden the field for research in hardwood management. It would also afford a wider range of possibilities in teaching and research in general Biology. Black Rock is in the oak region so far as upland hardwoods are concerned, whereas we have a strong element of northern hardwoods in Petersham. In the coves at Black Rock they can grow a much more mixed forest than we can here, involving more species of southern and central Appalachian range.

But we would have to take note of Professor Raup's caveat that dyed-in-the-wool laboratory men were "often afraid to work 'in the open field.'"

(2) The ability to do scientific work of narrow application. Here the case is clear that by 1949 the Black Rock Forest was yielding useful information about the condition of the forests of the Hudson Highlands.

(3) A tradition of optimism. The Black Rock Forest had, in 1949, a better claim than any other organized work of man, not excepting the Department of Agriculture, the Department of the Interior, or the Harvard Forest, in Petersham, to be continuing in an unbroken tradition, from honorable man to honorable man, the idea of conservation which Gifford Pinchot and others brought into American life in the first years of this century; which Pinchot articulated as an attempt to procure "the greatest good of the greatest number for the longest time;" and

which did not exclude from the work of conservation either practicality or science or morality or art or a sense of the spirit within a landscape but conceived of these aspects of human work and perception as constituting a part of a whole, which was life, viewed optimistically.

In 1940, Dr. Ernest Stillman wrote to President Conant, of Harvard, and sent with his letter a small essay entitled "Random Thoughts on the Harvard Forest," which included his thoughts on the Black Rock Forest and its future. He wrote:

Forestry practice varies so greatly, due to types of trees, climate, and soil, that I believe an intensive study of how to grow most rapidly the most valuable local species of trees on the soil available would accomplish the most good. It is doubtful if even our large corporations find that scientific forestry, as practiced today, pays. Certainly, the average farmer has little use for forestry. With the passing of large landed estates that is bound to occur, due to taxes in the future, and the economic necessity of more people migrating to the country, the question of the "Farmer's Wood Lot" will become increasingly important. What the farmer wants is an annual supply of fuel, with an occasional load of timbers. At present he obtains this by clean cutting a part of his woods each winter.

If, however, it could be definitely shown that by selection cutting he could not only obtain his annual supply of fuel, but after a few years have some ready cash in the form of "saw logs," he would be interested.

Two things must strike the reader. The first is how modest the goals set by Dr. Stillman were from a national or a global point of view. He proposes "an intensive study of how to grow most rapidly the most valuable local species of trees," a study that must have compelling relevance for a very few people — that is, if we are thinking in national or global terms. The second is his prediction that more people will be moving to the country and that "the question of the 'Farmer's Wood Lot' will become increasingly important." Would this prediction have been accepted by many men active in the world of 1940? I don't think so. Ernest Stillman was looking beyond the active world of 1940. And wasn't there a war in Europe going on at that time which absorbed most of the attention of many serious men? Was he looking beyond that, too? It is in the nature of the conservative forester to qualify every description of events powerful-in-the-moment, perhaps using the phrase "but even so . . ."

In 1949, Dr. Stillman died. In that year, the Black Rock Forest passed to Harvard University. An interesting artifact of that year is Black Rock Forest Paper No. 23 (Papers were shorter than Bulletins), which was written by Dr. Stillman's son Calvin Stillman. It is entitled "Economic Relations of the Black Rock Forest." Calvin Stillman wrote:

> Unfortunately, today's mature hardwoods germinated while Booth was plotting the assassination of Lincoln. Thus to be "commercial," a forestry project has to be allowed a very long period in which to pay off. No matter how much cordwood and minor salable wood products can be culled from a growing stand, the turn-over of the really valuable material is very slow indeed. Let us see what is involved here.
>
> Within the long turn-over lurks the very serious matter of uncertainty. A few of the elements are insurable — which are properly called risks. These uncertainties can be bought away by buying insurance, if it is available, with the new uncertainty perhaps of collecting from the insurance company. . . .
>
> With the long turn-over and the many areas of uncertainty arises the bald problem of the return on an investment in forestry. There is nothing intrinsically unprofitable about forest enterprises; other industries may prosper with more serious problems. But it is the bitter truth that when one comes to a real problem in forest management, with actual prices and costs, the conclusion becomes unavoidable that forestry is a safe investment only in the short run. In any longer period too many things can get out of hand; too few factors can be controlled; too few elements are even

relatively certain. Here is a very large area for research in forest economics. . . .

The considerations mentioned so far lead to the single proposition which will seem most heretical. This is, that I think the concept of sustained-yield management is misleading and, as taught, erroneous. The notion of sustained-yield management is wrapped in a aura of nearly religious devotion among foresters; it ranks high among their concepts of the good, the true, and the beautiful. It is understandable, therefore, if the concept has not been scrutinized with sufficient skepticism. . . .

Sustained-yield management, defined as long-run plans for production of logs or major forest products of any kind, simply doesn't make sense in our time. We can be sure of almost nothing. We don't even know that "there will always be a demand for nice clear logs," for although someone is sure to want them, we don't know that they will be in a position to pay what we ask for them. In short, we don't know what cost and price relationships will be in the future; we don't know what the demand for forest products will be at any level of assumed prices. We don't know what will happen to taxes, labor costs, and costs of forest protection. . . .

I submit that . . . the Forest should adjust to these uncertainties as data of its problem, and devote its energies to the one factor most surely fixed — pure science.

I now want to return to a sentence of Henry Tryon's, used by him in reference to the silvicultural work he was doing in the section of the Black Rock Forest called Glycerine Hollow. He wrote, "We may learn that we are wide of the mark or perhaps we shall be agreeably surprised." I want to put this sentence in contrast to Calvin Stillman's statement "We can be sure of almost nothing." I submit that the very different way in which *uncertainty* is handled in the two sentences holds the key to understanding the ingrained pessimism of the modern era. In Calvin Stillman's view, the enormous uncertainties of the modern world lead one to reject all plans the profits of which cannot be realized in a very short time — *before the world changes again.* Henry Tryon's work, on the other hand, seeks to understand (and to change for the better, if that may be) a particular situation in the real world — apart from whatever enormously powerful forces are at work (momentarily) in the world of men — and his sentence reflects this. Calvin Stillman seeks certainty, and finds that the idea that there is profit (or safety) in anything other than the certain ("the one factor most surely fixed") is delusion. Henry Tryon seems at home in uncertainty and finds that in uncertainty one may be "agreeably surprised." If we look at the mental events behind what Mr. Tryon and Mr. Stillman have said, we find that behind what Calvin Stillman has said is a fight for certainty: for certain safety, for certain profit. Behind what Henry Tryon has said is an admission that the battle has been lost: certain knowledge is not (at this moment) available to us; *but work can continue.*

Notice how the positions reverse: at first, it would seem optimistic to think that one could *know for sure*, and pessimistic to deny it; and yet if one finds that in one's fight for certainty everything in the real world has become unknowable or unfriendly to thinking-beyond-the-moment, where is optimism in that? And if, admitting uncertainty, one continues to do work and to plan for the future (a more healthy future, if that may be), isn't that optimism in fact?

❧ ❧ ❧

There was no strong interest in silviculture at Harvard at the time Harvard acquired the Black Rock Forest. The amount of money retained from the Black Rock Forest endowment for use within the forest was sufficient to keep the roads in good shape and to pay for the services of a part-time forester, a full-time forest technician, and a part-time crew. The forest was patrolled by a private club, which, in return for its services, was permitted to hunt and fish within the forest.

In 1960, Dr. Ernest Gould, an economist at the Harvard Forest, published an essay (Harvard Forest Bulletin No. 29) entitled "Fifty Years of Management at the Harvard Forest." In many ways, it follows Calvin Stillman's argument in "Economic Relations of the Black Rock Forest." Dr. Gould explores alternatives to a sustained-yield system. One theoretical course of action he describes would have had the managers of the Harvard Forest (headed by Richard Fisher at that time) sell off *all* the best-quality saw timber within it "during the high prices of World War I." In this case, he says, the surplus return over current spending could have been added to the endowment. He wrote:

Thus the fifty-year experiment in sustained yield has cost the Forest nearly $500,000 of additional financial gain that it could have realized had a different management program been followed during the last half century.

In 1972, when it appeared that a pumped-storage generating plant that Consolidated Edison proposed to build at Storm King Mountain, in the Hudson Highlands, would take land from the Black Rock Forest, Derek Bok, the president of Harvard University, appointed a three-member committee to judge what Harvard's position should be. The committee said that Harvard should take no position concerning the building of the plant. The committee recommended that another committee be formed to decide what to do with the Black Rock Forest and with its endowment. The committee itself noted possibilities. The committee noted that a private owner of the forest would find that he had a very valuable piece of real estate. The committee said that "selling the Forest in lots (small estates) of a few acres could raise a lot of money." The committee said that "Harvard should not think of doing this." The committee noted that if Consolidated Edison were to build its pumped-storage plant one good result might be that it could acquire the forest and give most of it to the Palisades Interstate Park. The committee noted that there was nothing in Dr. Stillman's will specifying how Harvard should use the Black Rock Forest. The committee said:

Nonetheless, Harvard should obviously make some attempt to follow the wishes of Dr. Stillman which, in so far as they appear to the committee, seem to be that Harvard do the best possible forestry research.

The committee reviewed the work that had been done at the forest (the Bulletins and the Papers). The committee said:

This work is generally rather pedestrian in nature, competent but with little that is novel or imaginative.

🐝 🐝 🐝

Now we shall look at the two chronologies we have set down, observing closely what *success* was achieved.

Looking at the major chronology (1892–1909), we find a record of success and failure mixed. Pinchot and Roosevelt succeeded in creating a system of national forests which was of wide extent. They did not succeed in their effort to create within these forests a system of work that would inspire a change in the country's attitude toward natural resources. Pinchot did not succeed in gathering science, practicality, and a sense of the spirit within a landscape into a conservative ethic capable of attracting or withstanding American enthusiasm. Science and practicality went out into the world alone; his conservative formula, "the greatest good of the greatest number for the longest time," was largely forgotten, and the national forests came to be seen as land that had been *set aside*. By the time a new conservation movement arose, the country had drifted so far into a pessimistic idea of human work that Pinchot's idea of *using* a forest was seen as suspect — a ploy, a compromise. Conservationists of recent times have perceived the flow as going the other way: not healthy modes of work from the managed forest out into the world of work but pollution from the world of work into the forest.

We now look at the minor chronology. Here we see the history of an attempt to keep an optimistic idea of work alive in one place: the Black Rock Forest, in Cornwall, New York. Here we must acknowledge failure. Dr. Ernest Stillman and Henry Tryon, working under the inspiration of Richard Thornton Fisher (one of the "closely knit group of men who helped Mr. Pinchot get the practice of forestry under way"), did not succeed in keeping Pinchot's idea alive on their tract of land.

We should note two small exceptions to the statement that the effort of Dr. Stillman and Henry Tryon failed. First, we should note that the money given to Harvard by Dr. Stillman with the forest did not fail. We may now look at a chronology of which money will be the subject.

Dr. Stillman established the endowment of the Black Rock Forest Trust Fund in 1940. During the period from 1940 to 1949, the income from this endowment was added to the principal each year. At the end of fiscal 1948–49, the principal of the endowment stood at $135,003.69. To this amount were added the sum realized from the sale of the Cornwall Press, which came to Harvard in 1949, when Dr. Stillman died, and the proceeds of three life-insurance policies that Dr. Stillman had made payable to Harvard. At the end of fiscal 1949–50, the endowment of the Black Rock Forest Trust Fund stood at $1,154,861.57. During the years that followed, the endowment of the Black Rock Forest Trust Fund was part of the "commingled funds" that formed the General Investment Account at Harvard. The General Investment Account was operated according to principles that have been described as "prudent" and which seemed almost to *shield* old endowment funds from the increase in market value of the overall commingled portfolio. A special intermediate device, a Gain and Loss Account, was employed. A capital gain, when realized, was not credited immediately to the various endowment funds; rather, it was credited to the Gain and Loss Account, which periodically (not every year by any means) disbursed money to the endowment funds. Thus, the funds did not immediately reflect any market gain in stocks or other investment instruments that continued to be held, nor did they reflect any realized gains that had not yet been disbursed from the Gain and Loss Account. Distribution from the Gain and Loss Account was at the discretion of the Harvard Corporation. From 1950 to 1970, there were four such distributions to the Black Rock Forest Trust Fund: in fiscal 1956–57, $121,329.36; in fiscal 1959–60, $133,462.30; in fiscal 1962–63, $146, 808.53; in fiscal 1964–65, $161,469.38. There were recorded as well two "capital gains" that reached the fund without going through the Gain and Loss Account: in fiscal 1951–52, $12,476.81; in fiscal 1952–53, $48.733.44. One effect of this system was to keep the stated value of the various funds constant over a number of years. The Black Rock Forest fund, for instance, was constant in the amount of $1,776,163.19 from the end of fiscal 1964–65 through fiscal 1968–69. During fiscal 1969–70, $45,785 was transferred to the fund from income. This was the only time during the twenty years from fiscal 1950–51 to fiscal 1969–70 that there was a transfer of income to capital. On June 30, 1970, the principal of the Black Rock Forest Trust Fund amounted to $1,821,948.57. Thus, during the twenty years from the end of fiscal 1949–50 to the end of fiscal 1969–70 the fund had shown an increase in principal of $667,087. Or, to show this figure as a percentage of the June, 1950, figure, the fund had grown in twenty years by just under fifty-eight per cent.

On July 1, 1970, Harvard adopted the market-value method of accounting. By this method, Harvard's endowment was transformed into something resembling a mutual fund, in which each endowment held a number of shares, or units. The crucial point, of course, was how many units would be issued to each existing fund. The Financial Report to the Board of Overseers for fiscal 1979–80 said:

> At that time [July 1, 1970], each endowment fund and each other holder of a share of these investments was assigned a number of units equal to its proportional share of the market value of those investments.

The difficulty was that it was not obvious how the "proportional share of the market value" of the over-all portfolio should be determined for the old endowment funds, since during the years of the Gain and Loss Account system the various endowment funds had not been allowed to reflect market value. For instance, the figure of $1,821,948.57, which was the stated value of the Black Rock Forest fund as of June 30, 1970, could not be used as the sole means of determining the Black Rock Forest fund's "proportional share of the market value" of the over-all portfolio, since the system that generated the figure produced a *book-value* figure that reflected capital gains actually realized and distributed only, and was *not allowed* to reflect the increase in the "market value" of the whole endowment.

On July 1, 1970, the Harvard Black Rock Forest fund was assigned Participating Units in the number of 21,712.1019. This figure, as a result of gifts and other changes, had risen to 23,907.3505 as of June 20, 1983, when the principal of the fund was listed as having a worth of $2,490,964. This amount Harvard proposes to keep when it disposes of the forest.

🦌 🦌 🦌

Each year, the Corporation arrived at a figure, given as a percentage, that, when it was applied to the stated value of the principal of the various endowment funds, yielded the "investment income" credited to each of the funds. The Black Rock Forest Trust Fund "earned" income at a rate of around five percent during most years. Over all, about thirty per cent of this income was spent at the Black Rock Forest and seventy per cent at the Harvard Forest, in Petersham. In establishing the Black Rock Forest fund, Dr. Stillman required that the income be "used to defray the cost of operating, first, the Black Rock Forest, and, then, the Harvard Forest."

⁂

I set out for Cambridge. On the way, I stayed the night in a dead small city in central Massachusetts, and the next day I went to Cambridge. At the center of the dead small city were large buildings around a square that contained certain official buildings symbolic of the life of the city. The official buildings were intact. Then, around the square: what had been a large hotel had shifted uses; what had been a large store had shut up. What was alive? *Embassies*: branches of institutions that collected this or that dollar from people all around the state, all around the country, all around the world, and had decided for this or that reason to continue a physical presence in the old heart of the dead small city. *Banks*. What was dead? The forest.

⁂

I want to return one last time to the symbols established within Biltmore Estate.

First, to *Biltmore House*, the imitation of the château of Blois. It seems to me that a great mainstream of American thought and action washes around Biltmore House. Biltmore House is *everywhere and nowhere.*

Within Biltmore House we may place Calvin Stillman's statement "We can be sure of almost nothing. . . . We don't know what cost and price relationships will be in the future. . . . We don't know what will happen to taxes, labor costs, and costs of forest protection. . . . I submit that . . . the Forest should adjust to these uncertainties as data of its problem, and devote its energies to the one factor most surely fixed — pure science."

Within Biltmore House we may place James Stillman's description of his daughter's Presentation gown, E. H. Harriman's assessment of the incoming Taft Administration, and President-elect Taft's remark "There is one difficulty about the conservation of natural resources. It is that the imagination of those who are pressing it may outrun the practical facts." That is, we may place within Biltmore House, on the one hand, the science and the technology that underlie the economic life of this country and the *practical facts* that are consequences of that economic life and, on the other hand, the unconvincing and dreamlike visions of *national life* which the national economic life has encouraged, and which decorate the national economic life and intertwine with it.

We may wish, for a moment, to take apart the *everywhere-and-nowhere* construction; that is, to separate the one from the other. The *everywhere*, we now see, is where the money is raised; the *nowhere* is where it is spent.

And now we are in a position to see the relationship between *everywhere* and *nowhere*. If one is living *nowhere* (in an imitation of the château of Blois?), the only pleasure is to be reminded that one is a part of something (even something as abstract as an economic system) that is going on *everywhere. Nowhere* monuments (like Biltmore House) are a rarity, and hold a fascination, since in our day the connections between *everywhere* and *nowhere* have been evanescent images. The idea that people once lived (or tried to live) in *houses* that were *everywhere and nowhere* must necessarily be very interesting to us — as interesting as the idea that a person might actually live *in* television.

Men and women who are content to live in Biltmore House are content not because they have found a way to live there happily but because they know something about how it was constructed; that is, they know something about what rules are in operation *everywhere. Nowhere* is *nowhere* for these people, too, but the contemplation of the rules at work is satisfying to them. Within Biltmore House, there is a sense of satisfaction that one is not, at any rate, bucking the tide. And if, by some chance, a person has been held back by circumstances from living in Biltmore House, there is a pleasant sensation of *joining* when that person enters at last. Some of this sensation is implicit, I think, in Dr. Ernest Gould's remark that the fifty-year experiment with sustained-yield management at the Harvard Forest "has cost the Forest nearly $500,000 of additional financial gain;" and also, of course, in President-elect Taft's statement "There is one difficulty about the conservation of natural resources. It is that the imagination of those who are pressing it may outrun the practical facts."

In recent times, to be *somewhere* has meant *not to be everywhere*; it is annoying to ambitious people now to be *somewhere*. The forest is inevitably *somewhere*, and we have neglected it.

Finally, a word about the *arboretum*. I have said that it is *here and there*. The balance of *here* is *there* — a place that is *here* to somebody else. The artifacts in a museum are, or have been, evocative of other particular places in the world in time. One important aspect of education involves the collision, in the mind of a person who has a sense of the place where he is, between his understanding of his own experience and his understanding of the experiences of other men and women, living and dead. Such a collision sends a person back to his *here* with a renewed interest in it. Such a collision is, among other things, a cure for loneliness.

The collision between *everywhere* and *nowhere* is no such benign thing. *Nowhere* threatens to obliterate *everywhere* in the mind of a person. When the sense of connectedness to *everywhere* is broken, even momentarily, the sense of loss to a person living *everywhere and nowhere* is overwhelming. Either a person's small space within Biltmore House is a vantage point from which he can see — everything; or it is nothing at all. Within Biltmore House, an interest in the way the rules work *everywhere* usually becomes obsessive, since there is no other source of nourishment.

🐾 🐾 🐾

In Cambridge, Massachusetts, I met with Mr. Daniel Steiner, general counsel to Harvard University, and

Dean Richard Leahy, who has as one of his special responsibilities the administration of those research properties appended to the Faculty of Arts and Sciences of Harvard University which are not near Cambridge, Massachusetts.

Dean Leahy said, "Various enterprises that don't admit students are my responsibility."

Mr. Steiner said, "It is that from our point of view, from the point of view of our scientific community in biology, it does not offer anything unique in comparison to a forest much closer and where we have a large facility. As a consequence, the amount of research at the Black Rock Forest is limited."

Dean Leahy said, "It is a division of the Harvard Forest, at Petersham. It isn't called that, but that's the way it is operated."

Dean Leahy said, "There is no School of Forestry at Harvard. Our work in forestry is limited. It is fully contained within the Faculty of Arts and Sciences. There are four men — two full professors, one assistant professor, and a senior professional, Dr. Ernest Gould, at Petersham. You really must go to Petersham. In addition to the kinds of facilities you'd expect, there is a museum, a dormitory, married-student housing."

I said, "If it has come to seem that, from the point of view of your scientific community in biology, the Black Rock Forest does not offer anything unique in comparison to the Harvard Forest, in Petersham, there must have been a moment when that became clear. Can you tell me how it was in that moment?"

Dean Leahy said, "It is hard to say."

I said, "But there must have been a moment of disappointment. That is to say, at one moment you thought the forest would be useful, and you accepted it. At another moment, then, the forest proved to be a disappointment, leaving you with a belief that it would be better to part with the forest."

Dean Leahy said, "Over time. It would be hard to pick a moment."

I said, "But men at Harvard found that the forest was disappointing to them?"

Dean Leahy said, "Now, I am not an expert in this aspect. My impression is that the soil condition is not very good. I think there was heavy glaciation in the area."

Mr. Steiner said, "Remember, we are a teaching and research institution. We are obligated to use funds for teaching and research."

Mr. Steiner said, "We do not consider that Black Rock Forest is essential."

Mr. Steiner said, "Consequently, we have been considering alternative ownership of the forest."

Mr. Steiner said, "*But* we have no intention of disposing of the forest for development."

Mr. Steiner said, "We have a passive, or neutral, stand, and respond to inquiries."

Dean Leahy said, "Bits of it that were acquired afterward might be sold separately. Where the forest manager lives . . . What we are talking about perhaps selling separately is thirty, forty acres, not integral to the forest. We are not talking about any kind of development. At the same time, there is a question whether

we ought to *give* the forest away. It represents, perhaps, the endowment of a professorship."

Mr. Steiner said, "If it can be preserved, and funds
can be realized to support teaching and research . . ."

Dean Leahy said, "We would add it to the endowment of the Harvard Forest."

Mr. Steiner said, "Perhaps a professorship in Dr.
Stillman's name . . ."

Mr. Steiner said, "One of the questions the law
deals with is intent. I feel a little awkward here, as
though I were being asked to be a seer."

Mr. Steiner said, "Who knows most about this? I
think it might be Calvin Stillman, Dr. Stillman's son.
Our records indicate that Calvin Stillman was very
closely involved . . . at the time of the transfer."

Mr. Steiner said, "Another thing is Calvin Stillman's professional training."

Dean Leahy said, "He's at Rutgers."

Mr. Steiner said, "In biology."

Dean Leahy said, "No, it's economics, I think."

Mr. Steiner said, "It was Calvin Stillman who dealt
with Harvard on the occasion of transfer."

Mr. Steiner said, "It is clear to us that Harvard is
not a conservation organization. Dr. Stillman understood that. The bequest of the forest is absolute. To
Harvard, without restriction. There is well-known
language to be used in wills if you want to restrict a
bequest: alternative dispositions of property if the
university does not carry out his wishes. He did not
use any language of this kind. It is a simple and out-
right bequest. No restriction. That says an awful lot
to me, as a lawyer. I think it would be wrong to make

an assumption that Dr. Stillman had required, or even expected, that Harvard would hold on to it. If I were interested in preserving a forest, I wouldn't give it to a university. At the same time, we've looked at the land, looked at the area, and it seems inappropriate to sell it for development. Although, under the terms of the will, flat out, we legally could. I will send you a copy of the will. My conscience is clear."

I acknowledged that Dr. Ernest Stillman and Henry Tryon had failed in their effort to keep the idea of conservative work alive within the Black Rock Forest, in Cornwall, New York, but we proposed to make two exceptions to the verdict of failure; that is, we proposed to note two successful aspects of their effort. We did note that the money given by Dr. Stillman to Harvard to support the forest and the work he was doing in it, commingled, as it was, with other endowment money of the university, quickly worked its way into the life of the university; and although its rate of growth has always been modest, and almost humble, certainly it has not been forgotten, nor has anyone proposed to do away with it.

There is another aspect of work in the Black Rock Forest which was successful. This is found within the Bulletins. They are octavo volumes, bound in green paper. They have on the cover the device of the forest: concentric circles enclosing the words "The Black Rock Forest Cornwall-on-the-Hudson, New York" and then, at the center, a depiction of Black Rock Mountain. They are well made and well printed.

Henry Tryon, who wrote many of them, had a clear, unaffected prose style, well matched to the conservative work he was doing.

Bulletin No. 4, "A Portable Charcoal Kiln," was published in 1933. It was written by Henry Tryon. The work it describes is, from a global point of view, *rather pedestrian in nature, competent but with little that is novel or imaginative.*

Aspects of local history are mentioned:

> Even before the Revolutionary War the manufacture of hardwood charcoal was a common thing in the Hudson Highlands, and in the Shawangunk and Catskill Mountains. The open-pit process was the method generally used until about 1875, when the appearance of metal ovens or kilns, designed primarily for the destructive distillation of hardwoods, liberated such quantities of low-priced high-grade charcoal that the operators of open pits were forced to discontinue except where their location afforded an unusually favorable combination of a supply of raw material with a nearby market.

A local condition is discussed; a tool is designed to fit into the local condition; the operation of the tool is described:

> Nearly all of the preliminary cuttings on the Forest have been weedings, improvement cuttings, or light thinnings, yielding fairly large amounts of wood suitable only for fuel. The market for such wood has steadily declined with the increasing use

of coal, oil, gas, or electric stoves, combined with coal-burning furnaces in residences. In order to find an outlet for our surplus low-grade wood, the local charcoal market was investigated.

The Black Rock Forest portable kiln is made of light steel, in two sections, with a coned lid. The bottom section is No. 14-gauge sheet metal, the upper section and the lid are No. 16-gauge. This construction was adopted because the lower section has to bear the highest temperatures and also is seldom lifted clear of the ground. The top section and the lid do not have to withstand such heat, and when the kiln is being placed over a charge both of these elements must be lifted at least four feet.

PILING THE MAIN CHARGE

Piling is begun with a double circle of dry wood placed vertically around the chimney. All wood is stacked directly on the ground and as tight together as possible. The sticks should be both selected and placed with care to reduce voids to a minimum. Follow this dry circle with the big wood, working steadily around the stack. The entire charge may fall down if the chimney be not kept as near the center of the stack as possible. Use limb-wood in the outer portions of the stack. Do not build the pile out to the full diameter of the cleared circle; it is best to leave it a trifle undersize and complete it after placing the kiln shell.

The failure of the Black Rock Forest was on a small scale; it was more to be compared to the withering away of a limb on the body of an endowment than to a bank failure or the failure of an enormous enterprise in which vast amounts of borrowed money have been sunk. One remembers that Harvard is now entangled in an enormous enterprise. Harvard has pledged its full faith and credit in the amount of some three hundred and fifty million dollars (an amount equal to the final goal of Harvard's recent fund drive) as security for bonds issued to finance an experiment (very novel and imaginative) whose purpose is to supply the power needs of a complex of buildings it runs in Boston. Here we may find the reverse of the coin: money withering on the body of an outlying project.

And success within the Black Rock Forest was small, too. And yet any effort that meets a certain standard of clarity and sense participates in the continuity of clarity and sense which runs like a small channel throughout history.

The writing of Henry Tryon, for instance — what can we say about it? It is *competent* and *pedestrian* — let's begin with that. As we admit that we look in vain for the *novel* and the *imaginative*, let us try to remember that the novel and the imaginative may take us in more than one direction.

HARVARD

There is now a publication called *Harvard Magazine*. The issue of May – June, 1981, had on its cover a striking picture of an old Asian man. His face was full of dignity. Half of his face was in shadow, lending a sombre tone to this dignity. There were lines of type in the lower left-hand corner of the cover. The upper lines referred to this picture. They read:

The *manongs* of California
They came from the Philippines to American farms. Their harvest was discrimination and poverty

The other lines of type were descriptive of other articles to be found in the magazine. They read:

THE SCIENCE WATCH: William Bennett on new cancer research
"The monstrous diary of a rather monstrous man . . ."
DEREK BOK ON BUSINESS AND THE ACADEMY: The use and abuse of professorial talent

The first page of this issue of *Harvard Magazine* was devoted to a commercial evocation of Harvard. There were illustrations of dinner plates decorated with Harvard scenes. It was remarkable that all the scenes were in the past. A scene of Harvard Yard in 1858 was the closest in time to our own day. Others were much earlier. The place of emphasis was given to the plate enclosing the most distant scene of all: a "Westerly view of Harvard College 1767."

President Bok's article, "Business and the Academy," dealt with a very interesting issue. The issue was: Should Harvard University, for the sake of money, participate in business ventures designed to exploit research done at Harvard in recombinant DNA? The article was written shortly after Harvard decided not to participate in such activities. The decision was not entirely a happy one. When Harvard is asked "Engage in business ventures?" Harvard answers "No." But Harvard looked at the suitor. Harvard noticed that the suitor was rich. Harvard heaved a sigh.

President Bok's article begins with this account:

> On a crisp autumn morning last October, I awoke to find my own likeness staring forth from the front page of the New York *Times* under the caption "Harvard Considers Commercial Role in DNA Research." The story went on to declare that the University was about to decide whether "to play a leading role in founding a genetic-engineering company," in which Harvard biochemists would use the methods of recombinant DNA to develop commercially profitable products. According to the writer, Harvard's deliberations were being closely watched by other institutions considering similar opportunities. A decision to go forward and join in such an enterprise would constitute a new departure in American higher education that could transform the very nature of research universities.
>
> During the weeks that followed, articles appeared in dozens of newspapers and magazines describing the merits and demerits of entering into commercial ventures of this kind. Scientists and editorial writers quickly volunteered their own opinions on the issue. Letters poured in from entrepreneurs eager to learn of our plans and to explore ways in which they might participate.

Once again, the *Times* had succeeded in transforming our quiet intramural discussions into a public issue of national proportions.

It may be important to follow the progress of these two paragraphs.

On a crisp autumn morning last October, I awoke to find my own likeness staring forth from the front page of the New York *Times*.

The pivot is in the crisp autumn morning. In that phrase is all Harvard to people who have been at Harvard.

I awoke to find my own likeness staring forth from the front page of the New York *Times*.

We have moved, quite efficiently, from the crisp autumn of all Harvards to the crisp autumn of President Bok's Harvard and to the newspaper that President Bok is reading. Notice that Harvard has been established in a certain way, President Bok at Harvard has been established in a certain way. Whatever happens now in the newspaper will appear in juxtaposition with the scene as it has been established: Harvard, autumn, President Bok serenely going about his business.

What has been established is: Harvard as a backwater; Harvard as a backwater with its own pretty ways; the world *interested* in Harvard; the world eager (and sometimes *overeager*) to report on events going on at Harvard; the world a little apt to intrude where it doesn't really belong.

Let us go on. For amusement's sake, let us *make up* a story (to compare with President Bok's) in which the great world will intrude on Harvard — with amusing results.

On a crisp autumn morning last October, I awoke to find my own likeness staring forth from the front page of the New York *Times* under the headline "Harvard to Shorten Parental Visits." Failing to understand the fine distinction we make here at Harvard between visits "parietal" and visits "parental," the active news gatherers of the *Times* had raised up rather an unnecessary stir, as I discovered when, ten minutes later, I suffered the angry words of the mother of one of our best oarsmen (stroke to our first eight, in fact), who called by telephone to announce that if it were true that she was no longer to be allowed to visit her son in his rooms she would see to it that he transferred to Yale.

Notice that in this story the world makes a *silly mistake* about what is going on at Harvard. My story describes a certain Harvard context, well known to its graduates. It introduces into this context a *flap*. It introduces people who do not understand Harvard and who may, through their clumsiness, cause trouble to Harvard.

Now we will spend some time with President Bok's paragraphs.

The story went on to declare that the University was about to decide whether "to play a leading role in founding a genetic-engineering company," in which Harvard biochemists would use the methods of recombinant DNA to develop commercially profitable products.

If one reads this sentence marking especially the text and subtext of the phrase "the story went on to declare" and the fact that the article is quoted directly, and not paraphrased, to what conclusion does one find that it moves? I think it is to the conclusion that the university was about to do no such thing. President Bok quotes the *Times* as though the *Times* were in error. And yet the newspaper was not in error. The newspaper had accurately reported important events taking place at Harvard.

Please see how the story is being abused. Which story? The story of Harvard in juxtaposition with the outside world, which I have epitomized in a story in which the outside world makes a silly error. How abused? My sort of story, a story of the old Harvard, is being used as a *trench* from which to fight a battle. The story of *old Harvard* has been wrenched out of shape to accommodate very serious business. Its essence has been removed, and it has been supplied with a new substance, which must pollute it.

At each turn in the story (for stories, however carefully controlled, reveal truth always, in the same way that posed photographs do, which show the aspirations within the pose), President Bok returns to *my* story, the story of Harvard in the age of airs and graces, and he does it for shelter. We watch as we would watch a military exercise — for this is what it is, within the context of public relations.

He begins in the sector of airs and graces. It is autumn, he is reading a newspaper. To his surprise, he sees his own picture. Now he is exposed for a moment. He must deal with the fact that a newspaper has printed an accurate story about an important development taking place at Harvard. He must proceed cautiously here. He may not say that the newspaper is in error, but he may put a distance between himself and the story. He does this by quoting the newspaper article so that the issue of Harvard's experiments with DNA, Harvard's interest in exploiting its research in DNA for profit, is emplaced within another issue, the issue of Harvard stirred up by the press, which, in turn, may be emplaced within still another, older issue — of Harvard and the outside world. The no man's land is the quotation of the newspaper article. If a reader is attentive, he will say, "Stop, stop. Was it *correct*, the article? Were you — are you — considering such a thing?" If, however, the reader is inattentive or if he is lost in the crisp autumn morning of his own Harvard, President Bok will succeed in transporting him over the dangerous patch into the *flap*. Here President Bok is on safe ground and may pivot back into the safe Harvard sector from which he began. Note that President Bok's treatment of the *flap* resembles the treatment of the *flap* in my story. He says that "articles appeared in dozens of newspapers and magazines describing the merits and demerits of entering into commercial ventures of this kind," and he seems bemused. He says, "Scientists and editorial writers quickly volunteered their own opinions on the issue," and he makes them sound like ladies in flowered hats.

The real story is the reverse of the Harvard-against-the-outside-world story. The real story is: There is no distance now between Harvard and the outside world; you could not find the boundary. The context of Harvard is the same as the context of the *Times*, which is the large context of the whole country of two hundred million people. The *Times* has understood the story perfectly.

President Bok moves from his discussion of the stir caused by the *Times* to a laying out of the issues:

> Eventually, after Harvard announced its decision not to proceed, the public debate began to subside. But issues had clearly been raised that provoked deep concern in many quarters. Should universities be more aggressive in seeking to participate in the commercial exploitation of the knowledge produced in their laboratories? Might efforts of this kind produce a new source of revenue to counteract the financial pressures facing research institutions? Could universities enter the marketplace without subverting their commitment to learning and discovery? These questions will doubtless remain with us for some time to come. Together, they offer an intriguing opportunity to discuss the state of academic science and explore the proper role of the university in translating scientific discoveries into useful products and innovations.

Follow the movement of this paragraph. First, again, the *flap*, which has subsided. The agitation has ceased. Still, there is deep concern in many quarters. Here President Bok makes room for what must already be in the minds of many readers. Yes, of course, people would be concerned about Harvard's going into business. He minimizes this existing impression by placing it "in many quarters" — which is to say, not in any place you and I know or want to name — and then he pivots away from the existing impression to an entirely different concern, which no one has voiced, which is: How should Harvard now approach business? The first "concern" he mentions is:

> Should universities be more aggressive in seeking to participate in the commercial exploitation of the knowledge produced in their laboratories?

This, I'm afraid, is propaganda writing. A person who is upset that Harvard might plan to go into business feels in reading it that his concern is being addressed. And yet his concern has been placed in a context he would not have foreseen. Let us say that the uppermost edge of his concern has been placed within President Bok's sentence, so that President Bok may say, "Yes, here it is," and yet one cannot help noticing that his concern is at the very bottom of the new context that President Bok is creating. Such is the ambiguity of the sentence that it would be possible for a person to derive from it the sense that people in some quarters were upset that Harvard had failed to be sufficiently aggressive in marketing the results of its scientific research and now the president of the university was being called upon to defend his backwardness. The next sentence does nothing to undo this impression; in fact, in introducing "the financial pressures facing research institutions" it makes a person think, Yes, really, President Bok must be urged to be more forceful in this matter. Finally, we come to what might be a concern of a certain group of people: "Could universities enter the marketplace without subverting their commitment to learning and discovery?" But that group of people is here a group that has decided "Yes, of course, do consider an alliance with the world of commerce, but make sure you don't subvert your commitment to learning and discovery." Anyone saying "No, don't do it" has to find a home in this group.

"No, don't do it!" people shout from some quarters.

"I know just what you mean," President Bok says.

"No, don't *ever* do it."

"Quite right. Without the proper safeguards . . ."

"No, I mean you shouldn't even *consider* . . ."

"Doing it without the proper safeguards, certainly not," President Bok says, and he walks to his conclusion, which is that he finds he has an "intriguing opportunity to discuss the state of academic science," and that he now finds, after this good, healthy, frank exchange, that he wants to "explore the proper role of the university in translating scientific discoveries into useful products and innovations."

I want to mention the Morgan Guaranty Trust Company here. Recently, advertisements for Morgan Guaranty have begun to identify the company as "The Morgan Bank." This used to be a *private* name for the company, employed by people who identified it with the financial patriarchy of New York. I think the name is being used *magically*. That is, I think that as institutions bearing old names go out into the world now they hope that by speaking their old names they will be safer. I don't think that President Bok of Harvard wants, any more than the officers of the Morgan Guaranty Trust Company want, actually to transform the world of impersonal forces and trends into a world of men (whose stories we may know); I think he only wants the forces to halt on command, to stop still at the mention of a certain name. The power of the impersonal world can be seen in President Bok's prose. When the world of men-whose-stories-we-may-know is not being specifically invoked, it vanishes from around him. His article "Business and the Academy" is peopled with men and women, but sparsely.

I want to discuss now a reference he makes to Pyotr Kapitsa, the eminent Soviet physicist. President Bok knows Kapitsa through an article in *Science* which gave a brief account, in 1966, of an address that Kapitsa made to the Royal Society. Kapitsa spoke, on that occasion, about his friend Lord Rutherford, the great British physicist, and about his association with him. *Science* quoted a little of his speech in an article just over two pages long. One of the paragraphs of direct quotation is quoted, in turn, by President Bok, as relevant to his own concern that the *morale* of scientists may be damaged if "the ideal of the disinterested scientist begins to be replaced by that of the wealthy professor-entrepreneur." Notice that Kapitsa's statements are as clear as glass but that to President Bok they are puzzling.

President Bok says:

Notwithstanding these outward signs of strength, one senses an unease in many scientific circles, a fear that the sheer size, complexity, and expense of modern science may have a corrupting effect on quality. As the Soviet physicist Pyotr Kapitsa once declared, "the year Rutherford died [1937] there disappeared forever the happy days of free scientific work which gave us such delight in our youth. Science has lost her freedom. Science has become a productive force. She has become rich but she has become enslaved and part of her is veiled in secrecy." The causes of this anxiety are not entirely clear. Perhaps there is concern that "big science" can bring undue rewards to people who seem more noted for their entrepreneurial talents than for the quality of their minds. Perhaps scientists fear that there is no longer enough time for referees to read papers with sufficient care or for senior investigators to exercise close supervision over younger associates. Perhaps professors feel that the direction of their work is imperceptibly passing from their hands and that research will increasingly be shaped to conform with restrictions imposed by those who control the funds. Whatever the reason, the concerns do exist and must be watched with the greatest care.

Notice. Notice. Kapitsa says, "She has become rich but she has become enslaved."

Bok says, "Perhaps scientists fear that there is no longer enough time for referees to read papers with sufficient care."

It is possible to understand events taking place now by getting to know the history of the work of which they are a result. The large impersonal forces that rule the world now were set in motion by persons-at-work. But it is hard. It is as though at a certain point records ceased to be kept. But that is not true. Records were kept, and in most cases we can get at them. The history of recent work has somehow failed to stick in people's minds. This has to do, I think, with the fact that the results of successful work are now dispersed throughout the world in such a way that they disappear; that is, they are not linked to any place. What will happen, for instance, when the financial life of the nation is no longer associated with *Wall Street* is very hard to predict. When the financial life of the nation is a matter of events taking place in the air (retrieved for a moment on this or that screen), will it be possible to raise a child to believe in it? It is difficult to tell the story of any particular event now because the old backgrounds against which a particular event would have meaning (Harvard and Wall

Street, for example) are unreliable, and yet they are all we have. That is why entertainment stories are set in the past, or are absurd and not meant to be taken seriously, or deal with some person's personal problems. To construct, through diligent thought, a true background against which events of this moment might be juxtaposed is the work of art now.

Since this short history of the Harvard Black Rock Forest has been difficult to construct (because the foreground and the background were being constructed at the same time), I should, perhaps, include a summary of what I think is important in what I have written.

First in importance is the *image* I put forward at the beginning. Two men, one a forester, the other a very rich man, stand on a tract of land. They first look at the land, which has been damaged and exploited. Then they look at an incomplete limestone palace.

Second in importance is the history of the men in the image: Gifford Pinchot and George Washington Vanderbilt. I mention George Washington Vanderbilt here especially because his idea — *to build a palace in America* — will always be a part of American life and should be accepted by Americans. But: he needs Gifford Pinchot at his side. In my image, he has him.

Thirdly, the various symbols within the Biltmore Estate: corresponding to what is *everywhere and nowhere*; *here and there*; and *mostly here*. I particularly want to direct the reader's attention to the difference between the qualities of the science of silviculture, which is embedded in a context (the forest), and the qualities of what Calvin Stillman called "pure science," and to suggest that "pure science" must learn from silviculture how to behave *as though it were* embedded in a context. The job, it seems to me, is to transform "the scientific method," which is free in a way that human beings never can be free, into "science," a collegial system that would recognize, as silviculture does, that life goes on in particular places and that "the longest time" is in fact the span of time we want to consider.

At last, the history of the Black Rock Forest, ending in the history of Harvard's unsatisfactory stewardship. Here, first of all, I would like to pay my respects to Ernest Stillman. In America, it is very often out of the work of men like Dr. Stillman that good developments are allowed to take place. Dr. Stillman held to the ideal of the *constantly flourishing* forest long after its *vogue* had ended. A specific proposal of mine would be that Harvard be asked to transfer the forest and its endowment to an independent foundation that would continue to pursue the silvicultural work begun by Ernest Stillman and Henry Tryon. No hasty action will do justice to what Dr. Stillman began — we remember that he rejected the idea of a private foundation because its plan of work would be "too narrow" — but I am convinced that the integrity of his ideal will be better protected now by a dedicated private group than by any large institution.

As to the *usefulness* of the forest: this is of two kinds — usefulness that was foreseen by Dr. Stillman and usefulness that was not foreseen by him. Dr. Stillman was right: the farmer's woodlot is important now. He was right: large numbers of people have moved to the country. What he did not foresee was that the scientific data collected within the forest might be useful as a base against which to measure levels of toxicity (in measuring acidity due to acid rain, for instance). And yet he did foresee it; that is, he foresaw that patient work within the forest would produce benefits he could not foresee.

As to Harvard's unsatisfactory stewardship of the forest: the weight of all evidence I have seen is against Daniel Steiner's statement that "it would be wrong to make an assumption that Dr. Stillman had required, or even expected, that Harvard would hold on to" the forest. There is a concept in conservative forestry called the Permanent Association. The Permanent Association for a given piece of forest land is that mixture of trees toward which all the various *successions* of dominance are tending. It is also called the climax forest. Such a forest, when handled with respect, will yield a handsome profit, and will return to health of itself: it is the constantly useful, constantly flourishing forest. In human affairs, it would be: a stable civilization. In America, this would be: a stable American civilization. It is my conviction that Ernest Stillman was one of those American men (Gifford Pinchot was another; Theodore Roosevelt was another) who believed that it was important to work toward that ideal however much the (so-called) "practical facts" spoke of its impracticability, however much promises of vast wealth spoke of its irrelevance, however much cataclysmic world events spoke of its smallness. Dr. Stillman, I know, thought of Harvard University as the strong home in American life of those persons who were working toward a *discovery* of what a Permanent Association for America might be. And, of course, it has been that (Theodore Roosevelt, Franklin Roosevelt, and John Kennedy are among its graduates), and it might be again.

FRIENDS

Finally, I would like to return to some of the questions to which President Bok of Harvard said he had no very good answers. Why is there "unease" in "many scientific circles?" What is the proper relationship between a scientist working at a university and the world of business? We turn to Pyotr Kapitsa's address to the Royal Society — to which President Bok has himself referred. Let this be symbolic of what I want to say to President Bok: You have good information close to hand, and you may still decide to use it. Kapitsa's address to the Royal Society, briefly reported in *Science*, appears in his "Collected Papers," under the title "Recollections of Lord Rutherford."

It is an affectionate work — we notice that. We notice that a man is speaking to other men, simply. It has great force. Events are not shapeless. It is a question of men at work. Notice the *pencil* of Lord Rutherford — how it has stayed in the mind of the great Russian physicist — and notice how the words of a Ukrainian philosopher have stayed in the mind of the great Soviet physicist, and how simplicity is not ignored. Mr. Kapitsa says:

Rutherford also liked talking about his own experiments. When he was explaining something he usually made drawings. For this purpose he kept small bits of pencil in his waistcoat pocket. He held them in a peculiar way — it always seemed to me a very inconvenient one — with the tips of his fingers and thumb. He drew with a slightly shaky hand, his drawings were always simple and consisted of a few thickly drawn lines, made by pressing hard on the pencil. More often than not the point of the pencil broke and then he would take another bit from his pocket.

A number of physicists, especially theoreticians, like to discuss science and apparently the process of argument is a way of thinking. I never heard Rutherford argue about science. Usually he gave his views on the subject very briefly, with the maximum of clarity and very directly. If anybody contradicted him he listened to the argument with interest but would not answer it and then the discussion ended.

I greatly enjoyed Rutherford's lectures. I followed the course of general physics which he gave to the undergraduates as Cavendish Professor. I did not learn much physics from this course since by that time I already possessed a fair knowledge of the subject, but from Rutherford's approach to it I learned a great deal. Rutherford delivered his lectures with great enthusiasm. He used hardly any mathematical formulae, he used diagrams widely and accompanied his lectures with very precise but restrained gestures from which it could be seen how vividly and picturesquely Rutherford thought. I found it interesting that during the lecture he changed the topic as his thoughts, probably following some analogy, turned to a different phenomenon. This was usually connected with some new experiments made in the field of radioactivity which fascinated him and he then proceeded to speak with enthusiasm on the new subject. In this case he usually put his assistant in a difficult position by asking him to give a demonstration which was not part of the original planned version. . . .

When I came to Cambridge Rutherford did no more experimental work by himself; he worked chiefly either with Chadwick or with Ellis. But in both cases he took an active part in experiments. The setting up of the apparatus was done mainly by his laboratory assistant, Crow, whom he treated rather severely. But I sometimes saw how Rutherford himself, despite his slightly shaking hands, dealt quite skillfully with the finewalled glass tubes filled with radium emanation. Although Rutherford's experiments are well known, I cannot refrain from saying a few words about them. The most attractive thing about these experiments was the clarity of setting the problem. The simplicity and directness of approach to the solution of the problem were most remarkable. From my long experience as an experimenter I have learned that the best way of correctly evaluating the capacity of a beginner as well as of a mature scientist is by his natural inclination and ability to find a simple way of solving problems. There is an excellent saying by an unknown French author which applies perfectly to Rutherford: "*La simplicité c'est la plus grande sagesse.*" I should also like to quote the profound saying of a Ukrainian philosopher, Gregory Skovoroda. He was by origin a peasant and lived in the second half of the eighteenth century. His writings are most interesting but probably quite unknown in England. He said "We must be grateful to God that He created the world in such a way that everything simple is true and everything complicated is untrue." Rutherford's finest and simplest experiments concerned the phenomena of scattering by nuclear collisions. The methods of observation of scintillations by counters were worked out by Rutherford in collaboration with Geiger in 1908. Since then more than half a century has passed and this method and the Wilson chamber invented about the same time remain the fundamental methods for studying nuclear phenomena, and only the optical and resonance methods for determining nuclear moments have since been added. And up to now all nuclear physics possesses no experimental possibilities other than those used by Rutherford and his collaborators. The present development of nuclear physics is proceeding not by the invention of new experimental possibilities of investigating nuclear phenomena but thanks to the possibility of investigating nuclear collisions of a *larger* number of elements; and these collisions are studied in the domain of larger energies which are reached mainly by the use of powerful modern accelerators. But even now the way which leads us to the knowledge of the nucleus is still the method discovered by Rutherford, and he was the first to appreciate its fundamental value. I am referring here to the investigation of the collision of nuclei. Rutherford always liked to say "Smash the atom!" . . .

Finally, I should like to discuss a question I have come across several times in descriptions of Rutherford's activities. The question is: did Rutherford foresee the great practical consequences which would emerge from his scientific discoveries and investigations into radioactivity?

The immense reserves of energy which are hidden in matter were understood by physicists a long time ago. The development of his view took place side by side with the development of the theory of relativity. The question which was not clear at that time was: would it eventually be possible to find technical means of making practical use of these reserves? We know now that the actual possibility of obtaining energy from nuclear collisions was becoming more and more real as nuclear phenomena were better understood. But up to the last moment it was not certain whether it would be technically possible to produce nuclear reactions with a great yield of energy. I remember only rare occasions on which I discussed this question with Rutherford and in all these conversations he expressed no interest in it. From the beginning of my acquaintance with Rutherford I noticed that he never took any interest in technical problems and I even had the impression that he was prejudiced about applied problems. Possibly this was because such problems were connected with business interests.

I am by training a chartered engineer and naturally I always took an interest in solving technical problems. During my stay in Cambridge I was approached several times to help in solving technical problems in industry. In these cases I used to take advice from Rutherford and he always said to me: "You cannot serve God and Mammon at the same time." Of course he was right. Once I remember Rutherford telling me about Pupin who as an able young physicist had come to Cambridge and done successful scientific work in the Cavendish Laboratory. Pupin was somewhat senior to Rutherford so they met only occasionally. Eventually Pupin turned to commercial activity in the U.S.A. and made a lot of money. Rutherford spoke disapprovingly of Pupin's activities. So I think that Rutherford's opinions on the practical applications of nuclear physics had no real value as they lay outside the scope of his interests and tastes.

In connection with Rutherford's views on industry I remember a conversation I had with him during a high table dinner at Trinity College. I do not remember how the conversation started, maybe it was under the influence of Lombroso's book "Genius and Madness." I was telling my neighbor that every great scientist must be to some extent a madman. Rutherford overheard this conversation and asked me, "In your opinion, Kapitsa, am I mad too?"

"Yes, Professor," I replied.

"How will you prove it?" he asked.

"Very simply," I replied. "Maybe you remember a few days ago you mentioned to me that you had had a letter from the U.S.A., from a big American company. (I do not remember now which one it was, possibly General Electric Co.) In this letter they offered to build you a colossal laboratory in America and to pay you a fabulous salary. You only laughed at the offer and would not consider it seriously. I think you will agree with me that from the point of view of an ordinary man you acted like a madman!" Rutherford laughed and said that in all probability I was right.

The last time I saw Rutherford was in the autumn of 1934 when I went as usual to the Soviet Union to see my mother and my friends and unexpectedly was deprived of the possibility of returning to Cambridge. I did not hear his voice again, nor hear him laugh. For the next three years I had no laboratory to work in and was unable to continue my scientific work and the only scientist with whom I freely corresponded outside Russia was Rutherford. At least once every two months he wrote me long letters which I greatly valued. In these letters he gave me an account of life in Cambridge, spoke about the scientific achievements of himself and his pupils, wrote about himself, made jokes, gave good advice and invariably cheered me up in my difficult position. He understood that the important thing for me was to start my scientific work which had been interrupted for several years. It is no secret that it was only due to his intervention and help that I was able to obtain the scientific installation and apparatus of the Mond Laboratory and in three years time I was able to renew my work in the domain of low-temperature physics.

I am sure that in the course of time all Rutherford's letters will be published, but even so I should like here and now to quote three short extracts which require no comment.

On 21 November 1935 he wrote:

". . . I am inclined to give you a little advice, even though it may not be necessary. I think it will be important for you to get down to work on the installation of the laboratory as soon as possible, and try to train your assistants to be useful. I think you will find many of your troubles will fall from you when you are hard at work again, and I am confident that your relations with the authorities will improve at once when they see that you are working wholeheartedly to get your show going. I would not worry too much about the attitude or opinions of individuals, provided they do not interfere with your work. I daresay you will think I do not understand the situation, but I am sure that chances of your happiness in the future depend on your keeping your nose down to the grindstone in the laboratory. Too much introspection is bad for anybody! . . ."

On 15 May 1936 he wrote:

". . . This term I have been busier than I have ever been, but as you know my temper has improved during recent years, and I am not aware that anyone has suffered from it for the last few weeks! . . .

". . . Get down to some research even though it may not be of an epoch-making kind as soon as you can and you will feel happier. The harder the work the less time you will have for other troubles. As you know, 'a reasonable number of fleas is good for a dog' — but I expect you feel you have more than the average number!"

You see what short and clear and fatherly advice he gave me. The last letter is dated 9 October 1937. He wrote in great detail about his proposed journey to India. In the last part of the letter he said: ". . . I am glad to say that I am feeling physically pretty fit, but I wish that life was not quite so strenuous in term time. . . ." Ten days before his death he did not feel that it was so near.

For me the death of Rutherford meant not only the loss of a great teacher and friend; for me, as for a number of scientists, it was also the end of a whole epoch in science.

Obviously we should attribute to those years the beginning of the new period in the history of human culture which is now called the scientific-technical revolution. One of the greatest events in this revolution has been the use of atomic energy. We all know that the consequences of this revolution may be very terrible — it may destroy mankind. In 1921 Rutherford warned me not to make any Communist propaganda in his laboratory, but it now appears that just at that time he himself, together with his pupils, was laying the foundations for a scientific-technical revolution.

We all hope that in the end people will have sufficient wisdom to direct this scientific revolution to the benefit of humanity.

But nevertheless the year that Rutherford died there disappeared forever the happy days of free scientific work which gave us such delight in our youth. Science has lost her freedom. Science has become a productive force. She has become rich but she has become enslaved and part of her is veiled in secrecy.

I do not know whether Rutherford would continue nowadays to joke and laugh as he used to do.

Publisher's Note

It is unusual for sagas such as this one to come to a happy resolution, but the case of the Black Rock Forest has proved an exception.

In 1989, Harvard sold the forest to William T. Golden, a man of intense commitment to science and the public welfare, who was at that time chairman of the board of the American Museum of Natural History and treasurer of the American Association for the Advancement of Science. He placed it in a not-for-profit corporation, which leased it for a dollar a year to the Black Rock Forest Consortium. The forest is now a 3,785-acre field station operated by the consortium, made up of twenty private and public scientific, educational, and cultural institutions.

Long-term management by executive director William S. F. Schuster and forest manager John Brady has produced a program that Ernest Stillman would be proud of. The research station offers year-round learning activities for students from kindergarten through the postgraduate years in a host of areas, from forest ecology to biogeochemistry to aquatic ecology. It features academic research programs on a wide range of ecological and environmental topics and also remains a hospitable environment for amateur naturalists.

For more information, visit http://www.blackrock forest.org.